Judith Beveridge | Sun Music

New and Selected Poems

GIRAMONDO POETS

Judith Beveridge | Sun Music

First published 2018
from the Writing & Society Research Centre
at Western Sydney University
by the Giramondo Publishing Company
PO Box 752 Artarmon NSW 1570 Australia
www.giramondopublishing.com

Designed by Harry Williamson
Typeset by Andrew Davies
in 10/16.5 pt Baskerville BT

Cover image: David Moore
'The sun and gum leaves' (1969)
courtesy Lisa Moore

Printed and bound by SOS Print + Media
Distributed in Australia by NewSouth Books

Cataloguing-in-Publication data is
available from the National Library of Australia

ISBN 978-1-925336-88-7

Reprinted 2021

In loving memory

Vera Newsom, 1912–2006

Dorothy Porter, 1954–2008

Martin Harrison, 1949–2014

and Bandit, 1999–2016

Other collections by Judith Beveridge

The Domesticity of Giraffes

Accidental Grace

Wolf Notes

Storm and Honey

Devadatta's Poems

Hook and Eye: A selection of poems (USA)

Contents

from *Accidental Grace*

New Poems

Author's Note

As a child, adolescent and adult I suffered from an intense and debilitating shyness. Apart from my family, and later close friends, I found it extremely uncomfortable to have to engage in conversations with people. It even caused me enormous anxiety to go to a corner shop and ask for an ice cream, or a bag of lollies. My first friend at school was overjoyed when, after many months, I finally said 'hello' to her in the playground. She was so happy that I'd spoken she took me to her home to tell her mother. Prior to that I would just tag along, never speaking. When I was older, I dreaded catching a bus or train terrified someone would start talking to me and I would have to respond. I must have often come across as rude or snobbish. Because of this shyness, I preferred to spend time on my own, which meant I relied on books and my imagination for company.

This partly explains why nature has been such an abiding source of connection in my poems. The natural world didn't make demands on me to speak to it, so I found much solace and quietude there. I also found that turning to literature and the written word gave me intense pleasure. I think it's no wonder that in my adolescence I gave my mind to poetry as a means of communication. I wanted language beyond the mundane. I knew how words had force; with the written word I could partially transport myself through my anxieties. I could manipulate words to sound more confident and expressive than those which I uttered under fear and pressure in uncomfortable social situations. I've largely recovered from my pathological shyness, but I still rely very much on the written word as the best expression of who I am and what my concerns and passions are.

I use masks and voices frequently in my poetry. These allow me to open up and expose my emotions in ways that are far more interesting to me than simply using the first person singular. As Paul Kane has said in his introduction to *Hook and Eye*, a smaller selection of my poems published in 2014 for the

US market, 'Beveridge breaks the normal rules of composition and, in putting on a mask, reveals something deeper and truer about who she is.' I hope readers of *Sun Music: New and Selected Poems* will find some truth in this statement.

When I look back on what are now four and a half decades of a life dedicated to poetry (I began to write seriously in 1974) I am surprised to see that my subject matter has not changed a great deal. Apart from the poems centred specifically around the life of Siddhattha Gotama, my main areas of interest have been the natural world, human character and places, and of course on many occasions, these concerns intersect.

I would describe myself as a lyrical poet and I am one of those poets who believe aesthetics are important, that an over-heated experimental or exploratory approach, or a poetics that privileges linguistic flux over emotional response, can take us away from the deep connection that language has with the body. I do not hold to the assumption that the poet does not exist, or that the movement inwards, towards subjectivity, is innately problematic. From the body we get idiosyncrasies of rhythm, music, voice, sensual knowledge, syntactical deportment, emotion and ideas.

However, I am also a dramatic poet. A large part of my oeuvre has made use of personae and historical characters, thus the dramatic tools of establishing personality, motive and viewpoint have been important. One of the reasons I am drawn to writing dramatic poetry and the use of character is the freedom it gives my imagination. I do not want to write out of the confines of my own personal history. I want to explore and investigate other voices, other modes of experience, to open myself up to new ways of seeing. Poems from my sequence 'Driftgrounds' from *Storm and Honey* are especially dramatic, relying heavily on heightened particularity. The drama is also a result of the subject matter: three fishermen pitting themselves against a harsh way of life – storms, rough seas, violence, the killing of fish etc. I have used a specific voice and character for the poems and I have amplified the poems' nuances and tones through their sound structures.

My writing can be kaleidoscopic, often baroque, but I hope also grounded and focused, trying to tether emotion to structure, image, cadence, diction. I am drawn to poetry that has rich texture, and by this, I mean poetry that is distinctly metaphorical, detailed, musically complex, but also clear. I would name Derek Walcott, Elizabeth Bishop, Philip Levine, Seamus Heaney, Donald Hall, Ted Hughes, Alice Oswald, John Burnside, Kathleen Jaimie, Sharon Olds and Carol Ann Duffy among my champions of this type of poetry, though my influences are essentially broad and diverse. I always endeavour to expose myself to a wide range of approaches. I have spent most of my life reading as much poetry as I can get my hands on, but I always return to, and value most, poetry that explicates Ezra Pound's comment, 'Only emotion endures'.

One of my joys as a poet is in trying to develop a unique relationship with language. Poetry is always inevitably an experience in language because no matter how sensuously, seriously or strenuously words may evoke the world – they are never the world. I believe poetry must always be a showdown between the word and the poet, that the writing of a poem should endure a costly process. I'm interested in the investigative shapes of poetry, how emotion can be dynamically yoked to form and sound. The poems I have chosen for this selection are those I feel best show the relationship I have formed with language. There are many ways to have a relationship with language: through form, structure, sound, image, sentence deportment, line – and this relationship, like that of many poets, has changed over time. My later work maintains a much stronger engagement with sound and rhythm, though still keeping faith with the image, but I have learned, while writing my later books, the importance and joy of using sonic structures to enhance meaning. I also use sound now as a compositional device, a way of subverting and distracting the rational mind. I find it hard to take seriously poets who say they do not consider music to be an important part of poetry. For me it's one of the touchstones for knowing I am in its presence, and as Robert Frost said, sound is 'the gold in the ore'.

In my work, I have been drawn to the long sequence. The sequence is attractive to me because it provides for an ongoing engagement with subject matter, and this helps me to develop emotional intensity and to build and layer character. A sequence can offer a framework for the imagination to slot into rather than having to face the blank page every time a poem is finished. I don't consider my sequences to be narratives, but more series of dramatic monologues that have psychological interest.

For this volume I've selected from only one of my previous long sequences: poems from 'Driftgrounds' published in *Storm and Honey*. My other major sequences belong to the two series I've written centred on the life of Siddhattha Gotama, the Buddha. I have not included any poems from *Devadatta's Poems*, nor poems from the sequence 'Between the Palace and the Bodhi Tree' published in *Wolf Notes*. I am currently working on an additional sequence which will add substantially to the poems about the life of Siddhattha Gotama. In the future, I will publish a volume containing this new sequence and a selection from the older sequences. My poems centred around the life of Siddhattha Gotama represent a different stylistic strand in as much as they are of a quieter register, and much more focused on the inward drama of the characters. I have felt drawn to this subject matter ever since I was eight years old and read about the Buddha in *Many Paths One Heaven*, a book I won at a Baptist Sunday School. *Sun Music*, then, is a slightly limited selection of my poems published over the last thirty years.

As to where my work may fit in relation to other contemporary Australian poets, I would cite Robert Gray, Martin Harrison, Anthony Lawrence and Dorothy Porter among my greatest influences. Unlike Gray, I do not juxtapose literal description with moral or philosophical enquiry, but I do often privilege the visual image and am keen on the way that description can be tonal and can gesture towards significant connection and modes of perception, though I am less of a materialist than Gray. I see nature more as a source of transformation and redemption as Anthony Lawrence does, and I also value the imagination for its associative and transfiguring power. I take enormous pleasure from the wonder of the natural world as do the poets I cite as influences.

I have loved the work of Dorothy Porter for its exuberance and energy and for the powerful way she has explored historical characters. Her seminal work *Akhenaten* was an important influence on my attempting to write from the perspectives of Siddhattha Gotama and his cousin, Devadatta, though our styles and tones are quite different. Overall, I am far less personal and confessional than most of my influences, less given to melancholy than either Gray or Lawrence, and less exuberant than Dorothy Porter. I've felt a deep kinship with the later volumes of Martin Harrison mainly for their exemplary use of detail, the way he brings to his subject matter open contemplation and wonder; his recognition that the world stands before us in such plenitude that our immersion in its multifariousness can bring both intense joy, and yet also a sense that we are totally incapable of holding such richness. I've always been drawn to poets who move through looking into vision, not of a mystical kind necessarily, but into some enlargement or transformation while still keeping tenancy with the extrinsic world. However, what really keeps me tapping at the computer keys is the challenge that using language precisely and in transformative and imaginative ways offers. In other words, it's the challenge of trying to write a good poem rather than feeling that I have something unique to say that motivates me.

There is also a meditative element to my work, perhaps more evident in earlier books, and in later books replaced by more dramatic polarities: beauty and ugliness, life and death, or by the task of trying to make interiority more tangible – but I would concur with the Irish poet, Michael Longley, who said, 'The poet makes the most complex and concentrated response that can be made with words to the total experience of living. For these reasons I would go on trying to write poems even if no one wanted to read them'. This largely sums up how I feel about writing poetry.

The poems in *Sun Music* have been taken from *The Domesticity of Giraffes, Accidental Grace, Wolf Notes* and *Storm and Honey*. I have revised very little of my published poetry, apart from removing some lines from 'Making Perfume', 'The Beekeeper' and 'The Eunuch's Lament' published in *The Domesticity of Giraffes,* and some lines from 'Hannibal Speaks to His Elephants' published in *Accidental Grace,* some lines from 'Whisky Grass' published in *Wolf Notes* and 'Grennan Mending Nets' published in *Storm and Honey*. I have made a few word changes, punctuation and line-ending adjustments here and there. Some poets remark on how hard it can be to make a selection from their body of work, but I found it quite easy and I chose to be rigorous rather than generous. One of my favourite volumes of poetry is Donald Hall's *Selected Poems* published in 2016, a slim, jewelled selection from his lifetime's work. I am not an especially prolific poet, though I do spend a great deal of my time writing, but poems take me a long time to bring to fruition. I love the polishing and editing process more than any other aspect of writing, it is here, working close to the forge, that I can get closest to sacred ground, to world-making, to a heartfelt engagement with the wonderment of what language can sometimes achieve.

I have included thirty-three new poems in this book. The new poems I see as an extension of my concerns and values rather than as a departure from them, though the style in some of them is possibly more conversational, and in others more tightly musical. There are a few elegies, but mainly the poems celebrate the natural world, or decry human insensitivity. I've never been particularly keen on irony, for me it's an emotion that is perhaps too easy to resort to and essentially rather hollow – readers may detect it in one or two of my new poems, but I hope there's enough overall sense of joy and wonder to override a creep into these darker tones. I thank all the people and poets who have been guides along the way, who have shown me ways forward, who have helped me to 'say the word'.

The Domesticity of Giraffes

The Domesticity of Giraffes

She languorously swings her tongue
like a black leather strap as she chews
and endlessly licks the wire for salt
blown in from the harbour.
Bruised-apple eyed she ruminates
towards the tall buildings
she mistakes for a herd:
her gaze has the loneliness of smoke.

I think of her graceful on her plain –
one long-legged mile after another.
I see her head framed in a leafy bonnet
or balloon-bobbing in trees.
Her hide's a paved garden of orange
against wild bush. In the distance, running,
she could be a big slim bird just before flight.

Here, a wire-cripple –
legs stark as telegraph poles
miles from anywhere.
She circles the pen, licks the wire,
mimics a gum-chewing audience
in the stained underwear of her hide.
This shy Miss Marigold rolls out her tongue
like the neck of a dying bird.

I offer her the fresh salt of my hand
and her tongue rolls over it
in sensual agony, as it must
over the wire, hour after bitter hour.

Now, the bull indolently
lets down his penis like a pink gladiolus
drenching the concrete.

She thrusts her tongue under his rich stream
to get moisture for her thousandth chew.

Making Perfume

So, that summer I picked everything:
the hibiscus that shut at six o'clock,
the white-pollened flower
I called The Baker's Daughter,
the yellow rose that lasted weeks beyond its season
and the great pale flower with a cold look –
Queen in the Tower.

Then I took some bottles from their cupboards
and their lids twirled off and their perfume
came three voices high in my head.
I lined them like wineglasses on the sill
and filled each with petals and water
and gave them keyboard names
like Chandelier and Tier on Golden Tier.

I remember how I lived that summer
in a room with a thousand windows in blue and green.
I'd stay out late to pick and soak the petals
and pour them into bottles and bury them in the earth
with a made-up name for a simple flower plus water.
Later, I'd wash and line the bottles on the sill
and read their labels until each one rang

a terrace of bells in my head.
I mourned the bottles I named for my heroines of hopeless love
and stood them in kitchen tapwater
and stored them out of the light.
I dreamt of balls, dinner roses,
a woman gently naming herself to herself.

Now, I wonder whatever happened to Lavinia,
the Fourteen Nights, Ballet Blanc,
the fragrance in the blue twirled bottle
I named Pirouette.
Months later I probably poured them down the sink.

But no one suspected that summer
why my eyes were suddenly circled with a dark pencil,
why my cheeks had the faint glow of day,
why I swished my skirts as I moved.

I kept the bottles with me, moved them about the room,
vowed not to open them for seven years,
and named them after the girl kept at home
who never stopped saying 'O, I wish, I wish, I wish...'

For Rilke

You can cup your ear in your hand
and hear your voice turn all light and clear
in its depths –
but we hear nothing, just the noisy world.

And the world loves to be noisy.
It loves to make a clatter,
to play itself with our tongues,
its diamond styluses,
loudly
and for long periods.

The world sets speakers above our heads
(even when we sleep)
blaring at tremendous decibels –
and we can't hold out against it,
in the morning
the words of its song
pummel our lips awake.

Our hearts – they're like utensils
taken from their original uses
and put into the world's jug band.
Listen to us: we are like bottles
filled to different levels and then struck
for our various resonances:

not like you –
your voice pure as a tuning fork

independent
of what it's struck off; the gentle
absolute humming of steel
against which we are, to ourselves,
severe grating, unbearable
dissonance.

Girl Swinging

A swing grinds on its chains.
A child sits pushing.
There's no eucalyptus,
atlas pine, or flowering ash,

no other child is calling
from the tender modulations of leaves:
just each note
of her ringing heart,
the feeling of being pushed
into the air.

I often think about
the long process that loves
the sound we make.
It swings us until
we've got it by heart:
the music we are.

But sometimes I sense
the child's life
twisted away from its
own mystery: the voice
struck, held back.

I long to be a symphony
levitated by grace-notes.

Quietly, I wait,
listening to myself –
when, suddenly innocent of misery,

that feeling comes
of being lifted into the air:
that clear singing
above bare stones, above
the common rattle
of chains.

Orb Spider

I saw her, pegging out her web
thin as a pressed flower in the bleaching light.
From the bushes a few small insects
clicked like opening seed pods. I knew some
would be trussed up by her and gone next morning.
She was so beautiful spinning her web
above the marigolds the sun had made
more apricot, more amber; any bee
lost from its solar flight could be gathered
back to the anther, and threaded onto the flower
like a jewel.
                She hung in the shadows
as the sun burnt low on the horizon
mirrored by the round garden bed. Small petals
moved as one flame, as one perfectly lit hoop.
I watched her work, produce her world,
a pattern, her way to traverse
a little portion of the sky;
a simple cosmography, a web drawn
by the smallest nib. And out of my own world
mapped from smallness, the source
of sorrow pricked, I could see
immovable stars.
                Each night
I saw the same dance in the sky,
the pattern like a matchbox puzzle,

tiny balls stuck in a grid until shaken
so much, all the orbits were in place.
Above the bright marigolds
of that quick year, the hour-long day,
she taught me to love the smallest transit,
that the coldest star has a planetesimal beauty.
I watched her above the low flowers
tracing her world, making it one perfect drawing.

The Caterpillars

On the headland to the lighthouse,
a brown detour of caterpillars
crimped end-to-end across the road.

Poke away the pilot and the line
would break up, rioting,
fingering for the scent.
Put him back, they'd straighten.
You could imagine them humming
their queue numbers.

I've only seen such blind following
in the patient, dull dole queues,
or old photos of the Doukhobors,
the world's first march of naked people.

I watched over the line for hours
warding off birds whose wings, getting close,
were like the beating of spoons
in deep bowls. I put a finger to the ground
and soft prickles pushed over,
a warm chain of hair.

This strange sect, wrapped in the sun
like their one benefit blanket
marched in brotherhood and exile.

Later, a group of boys
(their junta-minds set on torture)
picked off the leader.
Each creature contorted,
shut into its tight burr.
I could only stand like a quiet picket
and watch the rough panic.

I remember them, those caterpillars,
pacifists following their vegetable passion –
lying down in the road and dying
when they could no longer touch each other.

Reels

This one is fast, infinitely cluttered and agitating
beyond itself like an atom. And so, he has set up his rod and
his line as if there has only ever been the one Experiment.

—

A man casts out, in love with the long arc of flight.
This, the wing he can soar with
and assume a kite flier's attention to space.
But when the reel stops, he turns a sharp eye to the coast.

—

Will he be the runner in the long race
and the reel the slow, gentle runner on the spot?

—

This reel sounds angry – high heels on wood.

—

And this reel is sharp and quick and the beach
is the sound of a knitter in a lonely house.

—

At night on the shore under a moon faintly telecast
beyond the chorus of the waves
the reel is running its one thread
chattering to itself like a child.

—

In front of the lonely screen at night
he stands with the dial of the reel at his wrist
like a cracksman gentling his lock.

—

Slowly, deliberately as if a lens
were being wound onto a slide –
the reel is ticking, exploring the depths
with a hook. And he stands ready for whatever
shall be lifted up – as if a single stitch
were to be hoisted into the dimensions of a banner
and carried forward by a people.

—

This reel is an arrow clattering its target
and the man is lost
in the sudden unthinkable music
on a dark night, the surf breaking over the rocks.

—

Preparing for thought, for the long answer,
for a chapter's pleasure –
he stands firmly on sand, he baits the hook.
The lens moves slightly in its frame.
The hook gleams, the reel ticks.

—

But what shall he cast his long attention to
when he wants the tide to be understood?
He watches the sea run loosely up the shore and knows
the reel is the worried thought he must take into his sleep.

Japanese Cranes

Their frames –
an architecture of paper,
lightweight beams.

A low sun
huddles into fir trees, ponds –
trims the landscape.

Only the small,
or poised will survive:
such birds

of light breakable beauty.
Mating – they are
the original origami:

one unritualised peck
could chip them.
Such a skilled brittle

elegance. Earth can crack
its icy ceramic:
so their dance is brief,

a perfect choreography.
Their cries –
the rattle of tea-sets

kept intact
by ceremony.
And when they lift –

they could be glass
blown from a white
clear flame.

On Polling Day

They come from houses, factories.
My pen's busy over the page. All day
I add and subtract as on a bursar's ledger
those who belong to the institution of Australia.

We tally under grey-white collars
like enumeration clerks who settle our taxes.
But this is polling day – voting lines
trail like meal queues across the country.

I watch the people walk in: their faces
say you can pay and pay and still own nothing.
Fences and property-lines wash away like sand.
I am an official hunting out names like anthems –

citizen or non-citizen? – ready to draw
a thin red line like a blood vessel through the names.
But these are migrants, they know
you can deedpoll a name of its nationality.

For how many of us is Australia just a web
walked into from the old districts, shires and provinces?
We are all floated from a different place
we don't remember but still believe in.

An old man talks to himself, his face
shawled in his thoughts, memories of governments.
He offers me his name on a piece of paper
and a message declaring himself skilled

but of no property. I see them all come in
like blood donors. And what must I declare myself,
what colours – just throwing green into the sea?
I wonder about the old, true nation

that was once a dense complex of sites
not easily transgressed; the names of its people
written in the documents of dunes,
in old shells that stitched skin to the wind.

People, who when asked about their district,
could say: sand, wealthiest of roads;
occupation: walkers following the sun.

The Beekeeper

He hunts bees, those workers who dance
for pollen and wander incense routes
east in his garden. They buzz as they scrub out
their cells with the salt and chastity of devotion.

Later, they'll drool honey. Yet sweetness
can turn sour and today they have collected
from the crippled plum and there is bitterness
among the roses, mutiny in the hepatica.

He watches them enter petals like vestries
in which to pray. But he knows piety can turn
in a treachery of light. One day, they'll compute
the sun for an exit; a choreography telling them:

left at the rock, three times round the tree.
So he listens for them in their noisy gazebos
and ponders loyalty, servitude. They were hers.
She'd hold a jar of them to the light

small as dried camomile flowers; she kept them
among the cheaper daisies. A solitary man,
he remembers how, once close to his ears,
they sounded like knives in an attic of terrors.

The air leaked no scent of her betrayal.
Yes, he will rip up those plants. Now,
he watches for the queen. Is she plotting to leave
with the dance of another promised scent?

Any moment they could swarm. He'll burn
them, he thinks, remembering her lips crushed
against his, bitter as saccharine. His passion could tear
like a blowtorch through those racks of honeycomb.

The Herons

Then the path wound down
to a browner place, to a river
where rain-grey herons slender as rushes
drifted off like camp smoke.

I've only seen their colour
in a few opals baked deep in clay country.
When they stared, it was as if
their eyes carried on

through emanations.
One stood so peacefully
as if it saw and heard the single
far-off, crystal note;

slender, rag-thin bird we called
blue Gotama. We crumbled a mushroom –
all we could call
sacred, yet common:

but they looked past all hungers.
So we trod quietly back,
left them sitting above the long
brown earthworm of the river

and our pile of useless
vegetable soil. They were
beautiful as blue veins in the wrists of monks
fasting for perfection.

In the Park

Sitting on the grass
in the park – thinking about
what's going by, about
the pinks and plenary reds

of today's sunset.
Insects rampant as ions
off charged wires nipping,
tingling my legs.

Those buildings are like
bottles of scent fragile
in their lemon spray
mist and cologne light.

The harbour's becoming
dark against the chromocosm
of the moon adrift
under the stars.

A gull squeaks – it's
the sound of a pin
piercing polystyrene – it
carries out to the yacht masts

moving mechanically
as wiper-bars, out to
the Opera House, a cluster
of starched serviettes.

Now, out to the suburbs,
those racks and racks
of tinted light
rising behind the trees.

The Two Brothers

I just wanted to keep the snails away from those brothers.
The ones who, in the back garden, had shown me themselves,
grinning queerly as when they'd shown me lizards they'd killed
or sparrows they'd slowly bled with a needle. They tucked

themselves back into their shorts, next to their pockets
where they kept their things to torment me. I collected snails
and hid them in a neglected part of the garden, though always
some flower would let them cobble and feed at its stem.

The snails never needed more than a single leaf to paint
picture books for a child, the two wands at their heads touching.
When I picked them, they'd delicately immure themselves
into their shells. But those boys, big with the world

in their pockets, would dare each other any taste, any soft clot,
any ugly act. When they made tattered lace of a snail,
sprinkling it with salt, I clenched my mouth to my knuckles
and felt tears in the circle of my mouth. I knew this moment

as bitterness held to the tongue, as if next those brothers
would kiss me if I cried any louder, or told.
We watched the snails boil and froth like illicit stills.
They pushed twigs in the snails that tried to clamp

softly together, writhing with the salt (a brew those boys
dared each other, worse than the froth on swamps).
These brothers who had shown me the dead birds in their pockets;
how many grains of salt it took to evict a small snail;

the fate of any spider they found squatting in the loose shells.
But when they had held themselves in their hands,
they shook a little, not quite sure what they possessed
and touched themselves through the emptiness
of their pockets, scared they'd find the prize of nothing.

Flower of Flowers

A smell is rising from our bodies like a dark potato. We can't get rid of it, as if our hands are grubby with digging. It is in the wood, in the lemon, in the container of oils; damp and spidery, an under-the-house smell. It is in our clothes, in the fickle breath of the wind. We bring a cellar smell into the open garden.

We rub a rind back to its pith, crush leaves on our skin hoping its soaps will lead us back to a trellis of perfumes, the lemon to its sherbets and the earth to inodorous snow through which can leak only the scent of rare, blue poppy.

But wherever we go, on our hands is the smell of the dead unlifted to their graves, the smell of unpaid work, the kitchen smell, the smell of sinks and peelings, the cold smell of a stone turned over, the smell of moss, of drains, the smell of a stray, dark child wandering a bewildered corridor.

It is the smell of the earth raked, trodden-down, worked-over, battled-on. When we go out to the garden we feel like peasants whose bodies are the fruit of a plantation that is spoiling their whole lives.

O violet and mint, marjoram, palm-oil, cypress, meadowsweet, sweet cinnamon, calamus, cassia, olive oil, ginger grass, sweet flag and honey, sweet wine and almonds, tea tree, pimento, neroli and ylang-ylang which once meant flower of flowers!

The Eunuch's Lament

Outside, in the courtyard of the Begging Bowl pagoda,
peacocks mate. Like any upper-echelon eunuch
that terrible yin voice is tottering and high-pitched.
It is spring, leaves blossom like the mouths

of little dragons; green shoots sproggle
out of black earth. But a season can be brutal
as any man, any rough soldier. Perhaps, better
to be a silkworm than wedged between the Court

and the Bureaucracy just living for prize favour.
But thinner than a monk's prayer shawl, fragile
as lantern paper – favour will not last longer
than moonlight in the trees. So who wouldn't

pick off the Emperor's prize grubs
to stuff their own pockets with silk, to have
something to spin a life with? But what am I?
A boy poling himself off from one inhospitable shore

of memory to another, gauging a future
by horoscope, by season? No man drinks rice wine
through a pipette. No man picks azaleas of pleasure
where life is an orchid wasting its perfume

at the back of the Palace fountain. What am I?
A daughter with my sex unmanned? Will the wind
forever trail a cut voice through the waterlilies?
Will the butterflies, monarchs unto themselves,

float freely in the dusk? What am I, what forgery?
When a dragonfly hovers in the air,
the wind carries the voice's undanced song.
You can hear eunuchs fall with a scream.

The Fall of Angels

ending on a version of a line by Czesław Miłosz

Our heirloom faces cracked like china plates.
It all happened that day, at practice.
We were pealing off the scales, one by one,
when one of us bit into that note:
the high, high, highest E –
the god-note, monarch of all notes.
One of us, tempted too much,
inched his throat and touched it.

For a single second we all listened, stunned.
Then came the aeons of glass shattering,
each note broke a million panes.
We were shivering, trembling.
Music rebelled against us like a war of forces.
The notes annihilated each other.
C's killed C's.
Scales undid themselves like threads
pulled out of our bodies
and tones clobbered semitones from rocky heights
until nothing breathed off a dead scale.

When it ceased, our ears stung
as if they'd been tortured with electrodes.
We stood with broken wills and cracked faces,
our voices gone. Singers had become sinners.

Now, when we open our mouths nothing comes.
It is the grief of angels to have to belch
into each other's faces for excitement.

We are imprisoned in the gulags of dead voice boxes.
The voice is subversive.
The power of the note is absolute.
But people, we do not even have the hullabaloo
of many tongues to proclaim the mortality of language.

The Clerical Angel

My voice is a dizzy altitude.
I dream all the robes
of my hair are tied up
in a pin of anniversary silver.

There are so many obese records
to flick through, to file
at a desk overlooking
the slum-end of the universe.

It's too bad for an angel,
clothes stiff as lampshades
on a student's budget,
only a rope quoit for my hair,

God looking shabby in his
lab-coat, mixing chemicals.
I long to sing! –
but these days the organ-pipes

are test tubes and bubble without variety.
'Les Sylphides, Les Sylphides,' I hum
while God shouts back to me
'NO! the sulphides, the sulphides' –

his face deadly as asbestos,
running me from beaker to beaker
frothing with esters.
I must wait out the hot bouts

of the beakers, or till heaven changes.
I'm Pianissimo, the angel,
dreaming of halos, not halogens,
of Haydn, not hydrogen,

of key tones, not ketones –
my angst is so many angströms,
measuring milligrams for millenniums
and cursing the language.

All the chemicals in the air
have turned my hair (once
blooming golden under
the spotlights I'd sing for)

into locks gooey as mozzarella.
O, the days when the only
vibration that mattered was music!
The old gifts are lost.

Now an angel's voice rasps
against music like a bunsen
boiling dry a dish of pure water.
I long for the old order.

I hear the seconds of my life tick off
into gamma ray flak like a record
spitting off at the centre
after the song has ended.

And what does an angel do
when all he wants is music?
These days even the cherubs no longer
love their Cherubini.

It's Pauli now
and the rock music of the atom.
Planck vs Franck for the music
of the spheres.

Invitation

Cooking oil putters like an engine.
My kitchen is setting its course!
Islands of palms, dishes of singed coconut.
Will you kiss me when the heat steers east?
The pan dips low over soft island music
urging me on past salt and spices
to the ingredients of erotic cooking.
I'm reading the brochures of recipes
to impress with the wide map of my food.
I like the way a carob bean maps
the Caribbean (I will say) as we overlook
the harbour and Opera House (that rack
of draining dishes). I have bought wine
the colour of betel nut; all these fruits
are my map-maker's colours. We can stain
our fingers while the moon circumnavigates.
Already in the simmer of a kiss I hear gulls calling
over estuarine landscapes. I try to steer
the flavour, arrange the colours on a plate.
The kitchen is the compass sending us onwards
and it's nearly seven exactly.
Tonight, let's savour the place names of food;
let's travel through time like a panel of tasters,
we'll follow the tongue our native guide
and discoverer; whole tablespoons to tour with.
Islands of figs, oil carefully frying

a wild banana, a breeze gently rocking
and water murmuring like a slow sentence
lifted from the phrase book.
Whoever owns the language owns the food,
though once dreaming paths may have linked
our sites. We will stare into our plates,
call all fares to our table.
I light the candles, their flames
are the soft palms of stewardesses
in the heart's wild, imagined places.

Accidental Grace

When Will the Kennelman Come

When will the kennelman come?
The dogs are barking and the moon is gone.
The owls are out in the eyes
of the Doberman pinscher, hunting low.

When will the kennelman come?
Deep in the forest the kittens are lost.
The dogs are gnawing the soundless bone
as stars glow in a measureless paddock.

When will the kennelman come?
The bowls are empty and the shed's gone black
and the eyes of the dogs are scratching
the scents from the winter yard.

When will the kennelman come?
The kennelmaid has fallen over
the whimpering hound by the door.
The dogs are snapping at flies,

the wolfhounds are running the rivers
and lamplight is scourging the lake,
the whelps are baying like swans
nailed by their wings to the gate.

If only the kennelman would come
out of the long grass, out of the orchard
where the fruit's gone bad, out of
the shadows of the prowler's face.

When will the kennelman come?
And which one of you, my dogs, should I watch –
which for the scent of his kill
and which for his pitying whistle?

Occasions of Snails

1

They slide out of the light,
leave a chrome stain through shade on the brick path.
Their excreta are milled like censer ash
as they wander aisles, scented paths,
crawl over ageing grasses,
bask in warm mud like the terribly poor.
They wander the earth
as if looking for St Francis of Assisi.

2

So many anonymous buds –
a bucketful from the lettuces and roses.
The colour of autumn's loose litter –
they are aimless, evicted,
itinerant for the velvet luxury
of the orchid and lily.

3

The evening is cool, a cricket's call
fills the ground like a slow cistern.
I bend close to the earth, watch a tiny snail
rock in the crib of a leaf.
A trail just visible where spiders are tooling lace.
It works the abrupt edge.

It is a couturier cutting away.
It will quickly feather this leaf.

4

As a child I squinted for their script.
I searched the vast twin prayeryards
of sunshine and wind.
I watched for their headlines
as if they were notices for the arrivals
and departures of angels;
as if they were the proof –
beautiful and brief – of anonymous flights
scrawled across house walls, down ditches,
on uncut grasses, on a splintery fence;
as if they were the tinsels of a local moon.

5

Now I am a gardener.
I make their landscapes deadly.
I make Golgothas in the garden.
And I have laid my poisons –
the mockery of diced stems.

6

I have pressed them to the earth.
I have trowelled them into the soil.
I have riveted their pastel to the bricks.
I have denied them soft altars, plush roads,

these trackers of unattainable softness,
these evacuees of needle-thin tracks
who never look back on their painstaking silver.

7

But look how they go –
beseeching the deities Gloss
and Lightheadedness; how they stroll
among mucilage and essences
as if in mystical consortium
with nasturtium and rose;
how they find the sane bewilderment
of a child wandering her garden
with a rose in her head.
She curses her brothers
who drop them on cactuses,
turn them into sludge
and laugh them into sad weak bubbles.

Still, she remembers the hiss
of so many tossed into the ash.
Those winkled from their sockets by twigs.

8

Sometimes, when I hold them,
when they are immured
and smelling of lavender,
when they turn their dibbled heads

from my palms, I remember
those soldered paths
and this world's exotic itinerary.
Again, I track their rubbled passages
(to the roses, to the compost).
They have crawled into eggshells
as if into temples, as if into light.

Incense

for my father

All day a fragrance –
as if the sun has lingered too long
over the bowl of old green apples.
Outside the sun has turned the leaves
more apricot, more amber.
The sparrows are robbing the sunflowers,
a spider tools a web white as signaller's smoke,
and at the day's soft centre
the bees find the smell of burning leaves
to turn their honey cinnamon.

And there, clutched at by the vines,
the weeping rose leans
its thin frame into the wind
like a bare scarecrow, a dying saviour.
The leaves turn
their loose litter to the flames,
to the ash
at the end of the summer's reign.

I remember the leaves tossing
those flames outwards like garlands
and the ash that fell like backyard stars
along the tops of roses.

And that fragrance takes me back
to some sour nostalgia out of childhood
where urine and turps made violets.

The day we stood burning the leaves.
They shed such grey exotic wastes.
We watched those little suns extract fragrance
out of hard dead splinters.

—

Now all I have are these sticks,
pickets that stake out your memory,
wands conjuring old stars
and the air filling with the smell of wood,
of laurel split for fuel.

With these dipsticks I test the dark,
measure the oil left in the lamp
of affordable ruby – those roses
we watched the daylight dim by
as we fed their jossed blossoms to the fire.

—

You are gone, your ash is scattered
and these sticks just ghost your bloom.

But I remember the starlight,
the scent that trespassed,
the petal that opened, the red tip
that raised it all sweeter than it was.

The flames bloomed gold against the summer
and the weeping rose
we bundled into the fire
and all its windfallen blossoms.

—

In a confetti of ash and petals
I hunt out your memory.
In each decimal spark
in the moods beyond surveillance
I close my eyes to the tips
of infant roses,
to the smoke of burning leaves
uncurling like vines in an orchard
where light is the light of hillsides
in yellow May.

But in the betrayal of falling suns,
the thin stems eaten by red tips
on an insect timescale,
stars drop and burn,
tips grow amber with decay.

In a long red chamber
you are inner oils already burnt.

—

I watch the smoke move off,
it lifts like light,
it trickles like a hose
placed over a garden, over low flowers
that make perfect borders. I sit by
these stilts to stilt-walk in aerial wonder
at the earth, the water clutched at
by the vines, the rose weeping into the wind,
and the fruit fly circling
each windfallen length.

Girl on a Rooftop Flying a Kite

after Edward Hirsch

She couldn't remember what propelled her
out of the bedroom window onto the roof
clutching her kite against the wind

and the difficult angles, going high enough
to see the sun pour down on the dazed
harbour and boats forging up the river.

She put her back to the wind and unwound
a length of the flying line and tugged
the kite towards the first star pricking

out of its easy veil. It was an ordinary
February evening, the moon in its thin phase,
a light breeze spilling into the leaves,

the treetops rinsed in flame. She could hear
the hum of telegraph wires and the whoosh
of cars and the birds call like so many

Sunday bells. She saw the kite whiz like
an orange flare towards dusk's indigo stain
as the running twine pulled hard into

her hand before she could salve it
in a slit of sky. She couldn't remember how
she kept her footing among the tiles and

the weather vane polling each change
of wind – only holding her kite like a permit,
a chance for a flush hand, a ticket

to a far-flung domain where clouds pledged
themselves into her future like constituents.
She couldn't remember if the sun's final

reckoning was in gold or carnelian, or if
the shopfronts all glittered with the same
end-of-day scene, or how often the kite

snaked or looped before it lost its bow,
or what windows gave evidence smouldering
when the string grafted pain to her hand –

only standing there, looking over the roofs,
tallying up stars, balancing out her luck
in candidacy with the sun and the wind,

then posting her kite into a seamless sky
and her heart into a ballot of farewell,
her arms buoyed up like a sleepwalker's.

On an Evening in Late Summer

I want the bird with the key-maker's drill,
the chime-maker's hammer, the bird that sounds
as if a child with a piece of larchwood
hit icicles off a grille. And the man who comes

to sweep leaves from his gate, who feels
the shadows amass across his face the way
blowflies convene and scatter over the plums –
I want for him a sunshaft wide as a sombrero,

one he could nap under beside a stream
and a wild chrysanthemum. I want to put
my fingertip in the eccentricities of a web
a spider has darned in the Christmas bush

and free a fly from its orbit. I want to be
taken where the sun puts the scarlet note of
poinsettias into the depth of a quince-coloured
sky, where the fringed wings of the thrips

and the ephemeral beetles of this February night
go on in the mind of a child who finds,
in the honeysuckle and in the mayapple, a choir
loud enough to make her hum her desires.

I want to watch from the secularised regions
of the juniper a praying mantis step out
and tremble on anorexic legs as if it searched
for the chords of any diminishing number,

a psalmist trying to sustain a rhapsody
for Betelgeuse and the moon. What I want
is for the night to shake loose and whirr and dance
like a chanteuse of the treetops, like the bees

and the wasps drunk among passion flowers
as if they were the ends of bows zipping
across strings in a concerto; then, over
the compost and the roses – in études about

life versus decrepitude. I want the wind
to rustle the buds of the lavender and birds
to tin-talk with the rain and the fall of summer
fruit. I want the wind to call *esperance*,

esperance as it blows across the uncut grass.
And as I drag my bench across the porch tiles
this time of day, weighty with the calls
of cockatoos as it is with the perfume

of the gardenia, I want the fly to turn the world
on the turnstiles of its eyes, I want a girl
to turn plums in her hands, each a magenta sun,
and never need to wonder how far anything

is from a peer or a rival while she hums
her desires into the lobed leaves and scarlet
bracts of the poinsettias, her finger still
sealed in the strings of an immaculate design.

Hawkesbury Egret

I have witnessed your quiet flight,
the way you settle into the casuarinas
as if you had attained the sanctity of dusk.
I have seen your white tapered length
as no more solid than a Taoist's beard
perched beside the *Tao Te Ching*,
a stick of incense and a butter lamp.

I have seen those feathers evoke
the smell and drift of lemon blossoms
while the nuchal plumes paint two
brush strokes of a long river.
And when I enter the blue agates
of your call, I'm churned in a vast
stream and polished into a set of rubies.

Today I heard the sound of a little
bridge creak on its middle strut
and yachts sail out. I saw you gaze
beyond my shoulders at the sun
on a polished deck, at the wind lifting
gannets into a shipyard's trusswork.
And when the dusk broke your pose

like glass-blower's breath and I saw
you lift into a channel of sunlight,
I knew the time had come for the river
to take my grief and carry it into
the current like a stippled gem.
You flew over the water, over the moon
sinking with a show of bubbles, over

waves washing into a cove, over crabs
fitting back into their grottos,
over the river moving the greens
of a peridot into the low-lying bush.
You evoked again and again the light
of the wooden docks, the curve
of your flight dipping at times, as if

hollowed out by an undertow. And how
many times have I heard a craftsman's
meticulous hands turn his shells
to the light when you flew over the pier
and called for the fish that curl under
the stainless knife, or sound as if
wind ranked the sting of rockpools

in the cuts of the oyster farmer's
hands? How many times have I heard
the halyard ropes ring against the masts
when you flew the skies a sail-maker

touches with his hopes and needles;
and heard the coursings your voice
takes the river through, in the

prayers of a fisherman toiling
with a rope by the pier? You have
taken me through the eddying of my own
backwash full of rages until the yachts
moved in an upper tributary and I
could hear the lobstermen make way for
the headwater and call to the catbirds

along the shore and give two blasts.
You have taken me the way water does
an unskippered moon, fluttering it
back into a steadying beacon, until
it can shine again down the starlit
inlet where mullet-boys hum a discarnate
music, rev their outboards, dice

the darkness and sparkle the weirs.
And you have shown me sites seen only
from the willows where oystermen dream
the spill of moonlight into unending
pearls, where the skipper hearing
the catbirds again, dips his cap, blows
two more blasts and changes gear.

Marco Polo's Concubine Speaks Out

for Dorothy Porter

Marco, this letter-paper is pinned
against the sun. Where are you? Wind
is blowing in the chrysanthemums,
somewhere a chime drifts and a butterfly
luffs in the breeze like a sampan.
If only I could be on the harbours
where ships sail in with pearls,
elephants' tusks and hawksbill turtles,
but I'm here, weeping and tamping tears
on damask, trafficking in gossip
and opium. Marco, what shall I do?
Ruin myself with rhubarb and ginger?
Drink tea potent as dragon's saliva?
I'd rather sip the Chianti dispatched
from the ruined cellars of your gaze.

Listen, yesterday,
one of the Zambezi slaves, her hair
black and tight as peppercorns, offered
me this: *Pomegranates on a lacquered
dish pale as washed eggs*. It was
the coded news of the Empress's kimono
loosened onto marble. Marco, was it your
voice darting up like a dragonfly,
embezzling water from her Innermost
Fountain? Did you turn droplets into

free passages for the sun, each a profit
of porphyry and opal; or facet from
the luminous cabochon of the Empress's
smile some intimate crystal?
                    O Marco, be careful,
this Palace is headed by sexless men.
They dress as beggars and leave for
Omei mountain – and the Emperor's
displeasure can come like a whirlwind
from the Gobi if you don't return
with boxes of rhinoceros horn and
a ridiculous price for the porcelain.
                    My heart feels heavy
as an abacus. Who'll do its audit?
I wish I could be like the woman
I saw on the temple road to Tientsin.
She worked seeds from a pine cone
and gathered scentless flowers.
She lay with her face to the south
and traded sleep for the sun. I still
dream of your touch and of your kisses
pasted like slogans of oatflour and ink
on every door in Fukien. I shuffle
perimeters of empty days and cry
into a pillow book.
                    Marco, if you come
back bring some ruby-pink wine.

I'll bring goblets and kisses
more loaded with strokes and decadence
than the weasel-hair brushes of a Sung
Dynasty painter. If not – I'll make
a shrine for loneliness out of ylang-ylang
and sedatives. I'll blow dandelions
slowly across the strings of my mandolin
to imitate the cranes flying low over
Slender West Lake and over the Changbai
Mountains, leaving for the winter.

To the Islands

I will use the sound of wind and the splash
   of the cormorant diving and the music
any boatman will hear in the running threads
   as they sing about leaving for the Islands.

I will use a sinker's zinc arpeggio as it
   rolls across a wooden jetty and the sound
of crabs in the shifting gravel and the scrape
   of awls across the hulls of yachts.

I will use the washboard chorus of the sea
   and the boats and the skiffler's skirl
of tide-steered surf taken out by the wind
   through the cliffs. Look – I don't know

much about how to reach the Islands, only
   what I've heard from the boatman's song
and from the man who walked the headland
   to find a place in the rocks free of salt

and osprey. But perhaps I can use
   the bladderwrack and barnacle, the gull
wafting above the mussels and the bird
   diving back to the sea. Perhaps I can use

the song sponge divers sing to time each dive
 and then use their gasps as they lift
their bags onto the skiffs. Perhaps
 the seapool whispers of the sundowners,

or the terns above the harbour are what
 the divers sing to as they hold their
breath and swim the silent minutes through
 with prayer. I will use the gull's height

and the limpet's splash and the wasp's nest
 hanging like a paper lamp under the pier
and the little boat sailing out. Even the
 fishermen lugging shoals over the stones,

even the sailors shift-walking the decks,
 even the end-blown note of a shell levelled
towards the horizon. I will use the eagle's
 flight moored in the eyes of children

and the voices of men, the ones, they say,
 who've made it, though perhaps the purlin
creaking on its rafter, the gull squawking
 from the jetty, the wind calling

along the moorings and the notes the divers
  hear in the quiet waters of their breathing
as they seek release through the depths
  are all *I'll* know about finding the Islands.

Meanwhile I'll use the sound of sunlight
  filling the sponges and a diver's saturated
breathing and the wheezing lungs of an oarsman
  rowing weightless cargo over the reefs.

Man Washing on a Railway Platform Outside Delhi

It's the way he stands
nearly naked in the winter sun
turning on and off the railway
station tap. I have seen people
look less reverent tuning Mozart.
I have seen hands give coins
to beggars appear nonchalant
compared to the way his hands
give this water to his body.
Don't tell me this is a man
released for a moment
out of poverty, a man who wants
the penance of each cold drop;
a man who wants the smell
of his neighbours to vanish
from his skin, who wants to taste
what is beyond the scum
and effluent of the village ditch.
And don't tell me each drop
he takes to glisten his body
will never be neutral, though
he holds each clear spill
with equality. It isn't just
the water. It's the way his hands
take the water from the tap
to his body. It's the way

he attends each pore. It's the way
he decants the water back
and forth as if receiving
instruction for the repetition
of the names of God. And it's
the way he knows his poverty
without privacy – and the way,
though the water is free,
he takes careful litres.

Tarepati

He looks at me and I hear his breath journey
deep into the Nepalese hills. I hear it enter
the mustard oil he'd pool into his hands
to rub into his child's dark hair; her face
would be tinged with neighbourhood smoke,
her eyes with the snow and her voice would rock
with the carriages of trains carrying nutmeg
all the way to Gurdaspur.
            He studies his fingers
then pulls the dough from them, one at a time,
as if they were entwined with kite string
or the hair of his child; as if he wondered
when he would wrap his child again in his arms
like dark bread; when he would lift his voice
from these labours, his hands from the enamel plate
and call a child in from her game of knuckle-bones,
from her kite, from her flute of sugar beet.
            Tonight, if I were him,
I'd believe there was nowhere colder
than these marble floors; and I'd wonder
how much more this world could deprive me of,
poor of the train fare home. I'd be tired
of the wind in the dhotis and saris matching
my sighs and of the moon swelling with the milk
in the heavy pot and the spices darkening
in the hot oil. I'd be sick of the sifted phases

of my life and of how the stars seemed stacked
over me like household pots and tired of how much
bread I shaped for a moonless pan and of what
it takes to come up out of the dark and face
the light and work the flour, the wind
and the night and the stars of this city into a life.
            But he looks at me
with eyes that have kept their cool dark place,
their lidded jars. Then he picks again at the soft
dough on his hands and inhales deeply at what
seems a fragrance impossible to have stored
in a household he doesn't love. He lifts his face
as if to so many saffron threads blown into
the evening air – and colours the room
with the bright Nepalese sun that would shine
in the oil on his hands, that would lift
the scent of crocuses from the snow, that would
convince anyone he was happy with this life.

The Dung Collector

Tarn Taran Rd, Amritsar

Each morning she wipes the sweat that runs
from under the red dupatta veiled across
her face and lifts another load with a gasp.
Soon, she'll sit with her stupas of dung
and hallow the flies. Soon, she'll pray
each stack into the day's chapattis;
each new vat of dung into a tureen of dhal
to stir above the evening smoke. And she'll
work another hour or two raking the unbaked
yet steaming dung from the mud.
            I have seen heifers
given more freedom to wander the earth
than this woman who carries another load
to her wall then chants with the traffic.
            She could be any
woman humming at a task – moving a ladle
through vichyssoise in a perfumed apartment
off a sunny boulevard; watching light
slip into a room like a spoon into ingredients
for hollandaise sauce while she contemplates
the arrival of guests, the early yellowing
of the alder leaves.
            Clearly, though, this is not
about workmanship; not about having a thankful
heart in a beautiful place; not about

being a speck in the slurry of a rushing
Punjabi street, or about a woman who must
save herself by labour and prayers.
It's about a woman
who must live under the anus of a cow
as if it were her star; who must slap dozens
of discoloured moons onto the side of her house
for an orange sun to bake; who hears
the sighs of the world as her bracelets
slip up and down her arms like the songs
of insects in overflowing grass; about
a woman who bends to scoop dung into a dish
each morning with her arms and hands
and looks straight into my eyes.

Hannibal Speaks to His Elephants

Tonight when you put the tips
of your trunks in the air
to snuffle my mouth, my armpits –
I won't scold you.

Soon you will sniff the air
not for lions snoozing
under the baobab's cinnamon shade,
not for oestrous cows,
but for wolves
crouching along a frozen mountain path.

Tonight just listen
to my voice
as if it were a breeze ambling a road
in pitcher-carrying Swahili,
as if it were a gourd
filling at a well.

Tomorrow you'll hear
the chain-hauling, tusk-cracking
upward-urging commands
of my men
as if already
you trudged the ravines,

as if already
you were up to your tusks in snow.

Tomorrow the crags
will drive you
with their icicles and rocks
harder than the mahouts
with their hooks.

Tomorrow you will hear
soldiers in ice-crusted armour
clatter down a crevasse.

So tonight let's hear
only the tinkle of bangles
as if you were paraded in victory.

And when the moon
lays itself like a poacher's gaze
on your tusks, remember
fields of sugarcane and phlox.

Remember to bear the tips of lances
as if they were wasps
blown off your temples
as you wade the lakes.

And when you strain to excavate
a passage through the ice –
just imagine you're ransacking
something edible and soft –
the baklava and halvah bazaars
in Thessalonica.

Tonight let's forget about
the adder's hiss of the keeper's keys.
This is the night your trunks
could lift splinters from my palms.

This is the night
I could forgive
the days you muffled
the bells on your necks with mud
and stole all our grapes and bananas.

This is the night
we could sing the song of the bird
that scuttles up and down your legs
and picks off
the leeches and ticks.

This is the night
you could trumpet the air free
of jackals and tigers.

The night your ears
could wander the valleys like wind-paddles
where the Niger roars.

The night you could sing to the moon
as if it were the only jewel
ever made of your tusks.

And as I shape summer rain
one last time over your backs,
remember how I've taught you
to eye the summits,
how hunger will be the botflies
a winter in the far-off Alps
will launch towards your guts.

If we come back
I will retire you to orchid farms
and myrrh-scented lagoons.
I will put you in sunlight
along the Nile
and the Nile's tributaries.
I will let your ears be pinned
to winds drifting off savannahs
where you can snore
away your senescence
like victorious Generals.

Now I hear your urine hiss
on the sands of Tunis
and watch the scarab beetles dismantle
your dung across a dune
where I too will sleep
a campaign of cold nights.

So for one last time
I'll offer you a little
civilian happiness –
barrows of hibiscus flowers,
mud at a wallow,
the shade of the calabash
and sunlight
the broad river floats.

The Elephant Odes

1

O good humanitarians! You give of your dung like aid.
You support the charities of the scarab beetle.
You offer the puddles and gold mists
of your urine to the grass like oblatory wine.

You worship the water hole, the salt lick,
the piapiac. You open the long wet tunnels
of your trunks and apply mud (and if not mud,
then dust, and if not dust, then dung)
to your arid hides, free of all vanity.

You wander the savannahs
quietly as the shadows of Kilimanjaro.

2

When you are old and frayed, when you can
no longer graze, when your molars are worn
so you can't chew, when you lay yourself down
for the vultures and the botflies to luxuriate

in you like Roman tubs; when you bathe the earth
with your warm elephant-scented waters, when you wander
the forests for a place to lay your bones
in like scented lamaseries – then do you dream

of Sumatran rains where elephant-gods hurl
lightning from their trunks? Do you dream
of an elephant that carried a lotus flower and
a peacock feather in a silvery trunk, the last

incarnation before Buddha? Elephant, I praise
a senescence given to wanderings and awe,
mysticism and wind. I praise you for your anxious
benevolence, as if each one of you were a Jain

constantly sweeping a path with your trunk,
careful of microbes. I praise you for never
crushing with your stone-flecked feet (and for never
lifting a single muscle from the fifty thousand

that could dash into the teak) the mahouts who
pulled your bridles too tight, who flayed your ears
with hooks, who cut their commands with chains
and whips, who overcrowded your howdahs.

3

I praise your sagacity, your amiability.
I praise you when you come walking under
monkey bread trees flushed with light,
patched with shadow; when you come
floating along the edges of water holes,
when you amble out of acacia forests

powdered with pollen, or when you
snuffle the dirt and open your throat
and trumpet; when you curl your trunk
into your keeper's hand grateful
he doesn't weigh the white bullion
of your tusks with his human eyes.

4

You have never fostered
the fractious, uppity jaunt of the camel,
or the lubricious saunter of the horse.

You haven't become solitary
and depraved like the rhino,
that crazed commando, staking out the shadows,
plotting its aristocracy from a tooth.

You have never become mean like the mule;
you have never given in to buffoonery like the hippo,
or to asceticism like the yak,
or to hubris like the lion,
or to anorexia nervosa like the giraffe,
or to peccancy like the pig.
Not even to obsequiousness
like the jackal howling *bwana bwana*
at death for a corpse.

5

I praise your strength, your ambulant
astrologies, the deft wisdom
of your trunks sensitive as pipettes.
I praise your temples
when they drip with musth, when they are
covered with aphids and wasps. I praise you
lumbering to bathe, each a Tiresias.

6

When you dream, closing your Homeric eyelids,
do you fall into a pit and enter the catacombs
of species-memory? Do you shudder hearing
battle cries? Do your feet trace out
manoeuvres of prudent warfare, or the steps
of the Watusi on a tightrope in a circus?
Or do they trace the mincing choreodramas
with which your copulations entertained
the Maharajas?

Or do they stampede from
the guns of ivory hunters who in a single
decade halved your populations? *There is*
nothing more satisfying than the complete
flop of an elephant shot in the head.

Or do they twitch for
the impala's flight, the gazelle's leap,
longing to be hoofed, longing to be

swift across the grass, longing for the steps
of a lunar heart? Or do they wish
to be belled and trinketed,
to tread on temple orchids, to stand
in rows in scented halls where
a woman sings all her elephants to sleep?

7

In the valleys at night, the last birds
calling in the distance like crepuscular flutes –
imagine, then, how each poor elephant
must be ballooned and bloated:

all that xylem and phloem
mixing into a grand epic,
and the accompaniment! – flugelhorn and hecklephone,
woodwind and bass clarinet
and the rumble-seated jeepney –

and each elephant an audience
in a separate marquee, a Count Basie
on a stage –
and they are waiting, waiting
for the trombone, only the trombone! –
all night bellowing,
bellowing to the god
with which they are afflated.

8

And as you mount the teak platform
and accept without perturbation
the King's ministrations,

I wonder how long
you will survive
tied to the scented dais,
shaded with silk,
given jasmine showers,
fed platters of delicacies?

I wonder how long before your pale green eyes
focus into the moons of your toenails?

O Carrier of Vishnu
O One the Colour of Water Lotus
O One Born of Clouds and Rain
O Most Beautiful and Rare of All –

the King has fed you sugarcane
that has your name
carved into the stalk
in a delicate script

and you have been certified
by the Seven Measures
of Elephant Whiteness

and proclaimed by
the Most High and Renowned
of all Elephant Metaphysicians
to be the descendant
of the winged elephant
who roamed the cloudscapes,
avatar of Buddha.

9

Sometimes, when I dream,
I am the soft-nosed, arrow-struck,
tooth-poached one. I am the one
dragging my starved belly
through deracinated fields,
prowling and grieving and lifting

the bones of my loved ones
and weeping. I am the one
beseeching my enemy not to make
a trench in the earth with me,
not to pulp me, not to skin me
rolling me with his feet, not

to enter arenas and colosseums
and hurl the javelin. Then –
you come to my nightmare gently
and tap my forehead with your

trunk and you calm me with your
Ganesh-wise eyes and offer me

the granite step-up of your knee –
so that in the sudden limber lift
out of my nightmare's pit
I can see your pointed moons
brandish towards the enemy.
I can see the property of Heaven.

10

What news can you bring us
of the earth?

We are shut off
between the hummingbirds
and the earless snakes.

But you!
when your big ears flap,
you are the Hearers

of all
the poetry of the earth.

Yachts

They are the sound of teacups wheeled off,
of a blackbutt's littlest birds rattling
song-bottles in all its sun-tiered racks.

And if you can imagine brittle bells
fiddled with and shaken, if you can hear
a woman placing her earrings in a pearl

shell, if you can hear the chime from
a lacquered box at the gateway to a palace,
if you can hear the feet of a bird on tin

shingles in the depth of an agate sky,
then you'll know too the sound of a latch
dropping shut, and you'll know the little

shovelfuls of laughter children scatter
on the grass. You'll know the call
of an oriole on a lakeside walk and how

rain drips from branch to branch in bushes
that have broken out in buds. And you
might even know, some evening when

the weather's calm, the sky still blue,
how a child drops a soupspoon in a dish.
Or you might hear the bird, the one that

calls to whoever sits on the porch on
a summer's night and listens to the tripping
of bells from a bay, having already

struggled up a precipitous pass
and dared difficult, sultry questions
with their face open to the sea.

Maybe you only hear yourself stumble
up a staircase and drop your keys. Maybe
you only hear the sharp strike-notes

of bellringers announcing the passing
of another life, or hear your name on
the lips of sailors who sit with spray

on their fingers as they pull in the weights
and chip and chisel into the night.
Perhaps you hear your life winched in

under a dying sun. Or perhaps you hear
a child count stars in the water off a rickety
pier – despite clouds moving in, despite

gulls in the wind just off the masts.

How to Love Bats

Begin in a cave.
Listen to the floor boil with rodents, insects.
Weep for the pups that have fallen. Later,
you'll fly the narrow passages of those bones, but for now –

open your mouth, out will fly names
like *Pipistrelle*, *Desmodus*, *Tadarida*. Then,
listen for a frequency
lower than the seep of water, higher
than an ice planet hibernating
beyond a glacier of Time.

Visit op shops. Hide in their closets.
Breathe in the scales and dust
of clothes left hanging. To the underwear
and to the crumpled black silks – well,
give them your imagination
and plenty of line, also a night of gentle wind.

By now your fingers should have
touched petals open. You should have been dreaming
each night of anthers and of giving
to their furred beauty
your nectar-loving tongue. But also,
your tongue should have been practising the cold
of a slippery, frog-filled pond.

Go down on your elbows and knees.
You'll need a speleologist's desire for rebirth
and a miner's paranoia of gases –
but try to find within yourself
the scent of a bat-loving flower.

Read books on pogroms. Never trust an owl.
Its face is the biography of propaganda.
Never trust a hawk. See its solutions
in the fur and bones of regurgitated pellets.

And have you considered the smoke
yet from a moving train? You can start
half an hour before sunset,
but make sure the journey is long, uninterrupted
and that you never discover
the faces of those trans-Siberian exiles.

Spend time in the folds of curtains.
Seek out boarding school cloakrooms.
Practise the gymnastics of wet umbrellas.

                Are you
floating yet, thought-light,
without a keel on your breastbone?
Then, meditate on your bones as piccolos,
on mastering the thermals

beyond the tremolo; reverberations
beyond the lexical.

                Become adept
at describing the spectacles of the echo –
but don't watch dark clouds
passing across the moon. This may lead you
to fetishes and cults that worship false gods
by lapping up bowls of blood from a tomb.

Practise echo locating aerodromes,
stamens. Send out rippling octaves
into the fossils of dank caves –
then edit these soundtracks
with a metronome of dripping rocks, heartbeats
and with a continuous, high-scaled wondering
about the evolution of your own mind.

But look, I must tell you – these instructions
are no manual. Months of practice
may still only win you appreciation
of the acoustical moth,
hatred of the hawk and owl. You may need

to observe further the floating black host
through the hills.

Naming Roses

This one is called *Grandchild*, this *Happy Days*,
this one is *Soliloquy*, this is *Crosby*
and this one – *Maria Callas*.
Blossoms of light they stand, idle and blessed
like luminaries. Soon, in her hands she will hold
the spent petals, the public scents –

but for a moment she pauses,
lifts her head – as if some perfume
takes her back through open gardens and doors –
to a woman holding roses close to her face,

a bright red bunch given to her
with words and sweet breath,
with promises and days to order
with wine and the music of venues and events.
She hears the music she would love to sing to
as she pauses over the roses, and her life

is no longer here in this chill afternoon garden,
but is a fragrance that travels incognito
in her hands: singular and rare.
She intones the idol in each unhurried petal
and listens to the ways some days are shaped:
Rendezvous, Soirée, Tête-à-Tête

and all the paths are full that fill
the intimate fragrance of her life:
each rose a door swinging open
as she strays then leaves, room by room, for the night –
whispering *Cheer*, *Fiesta*, *Camaraderie*
as if she knew she would never be more alone than she wanted;
past *Stage Door*, *Recital*, *Double Ovation* –
as if roses would always be giving their lives
and their small performances;
as if she would always
be bending to roses on calm clear nights,
as if each were the stairway out of a stuffy house.

And by bending close
to the pure fragrance of her life
she could sing any song she wanted, any way she chose.

Wolf Notes

Bahadour

The sun stamps his shadow on the wall
and he's left one wheel of his bicycle
spinning. It is dusk, there are a few minutes

before he must pedal his wares through
the streets again. But now, nothing
is more important than his kite working

its way into the wobbly winter sky.
For the time he can live at the summit
of his head without a ticket, he is following

the kite through pastures of snow where
his father calls into the mountains for him,
where his mother weeps his farewell into

the carriages of a five-day train. You can
see so many boys out on the rooftops this time
of day, surrendering diamonds to

the thin blue air, putting their arms up, neither
in answer nor apprehension, but because
the day tenders them a coupon of release.

He does not think about the failing light,
nor of how his legs must mint so many steel
suns from a bicycle's wheels each day,

nor of how his life must drop like a token
into its appropriate slot; not even
of constructing whatever angles would break

the deal that transacted away his childhood,
nor of taking some fairness back to Nepal –
but only of how he can find purchase

with whatever minutes of dusk are left
to raise a diamond, to claim some share
of hope, some acre of sky within a hard-fisted

budget; and of how happy he is, yielding,
his arms up, equivalent now only to himself,
a last spoke in the denominations of light.

The Saffron Picker

To produce one kilogram of saffron, it
is necessary to pick 150,000 crocuses

Soon, she'll crouch again above each crocus,
feel how the scales set by fate, by misfortune
are an awesome tonnage: a weight opposing

time. Soon, the sun will transpose its shadows
onto the faces of her children. She knows
equations: how many stigmas balance each

day with the next; how many days divvy up
the one meal; how many rounds of a lustrous
table the sun must go before enough yellow

makes a spoonful heavy. She spreads a cloth,
calls to the competing zeroes of her children's
mouths. An apronful becomes her standard –

and those purple fields of unfair equivalence.
Always that weight in her apron: the indivisible
hunger that never has the levity of flowers.

The Dice-Player

I've had my nose in the ring since I was nine.
I learned those cubes fast: how to play a blind
bargain; how to empty a die from my palm
and beguile by turns loaded with prayers –
then sleight of hand. Ten or fifteen years
and you get wrists like a tabla-player's, jaws

cut and edged by the knuckles and customs
of luck and deception. The fun's in sham,
in subterfuge, in the eyes smoking out
an opponent's call. I let my thumb stalk
each die, get to know which edge might
damage probability's well-worn curves.

See, all dice are cut on the teeth of thugs,
liars and raconteurs. I've concocted calls
those dealing in risk and perfidy, bluff or
perjury, would envy. But I've never stolen
or coveted dice fashioned from agate
or amber, slate or jasper, or from

the perfumed peach stones of distant shores.
Some think fortunes will be won with dice
made from the regurgitated pellets of owls;
or from the guano of seabirds that ride only

the loftiest thermals. I've always had faith
in the anklebones of goats, in the luxated

kneecaps of mountain-loving pugs. Look,
I've wagered all my life on the belief that
I can dupe the stars, subtend the arcs, turn
out *scrolls, louvres, pups, knacks, double*
demons – well, at least give a game rhythm.
I know there'll always be an affliction

of black spots before my eyes, that my face
has its smile stacked slightly higher on
the one side, that the odds I'm not a swindler
are never square. But, Sir, when some rough
justice gets me back again to the floor,
then watch me throw fate a weighted side.

Pedlar

Sure, I've haggled on corners with fruiterers,
barrowboys raising phlegm. I've gone on
day after day, putting forward a face I know

to be long ago cashiered of its gloss. Some
days I've buffed my face with a less penniless
tarnish and walked out into daylight's lucrative

polish. These days who knows what's delusively
real from what's genuinely ersatz. I've carried
the faked weight of my voice through these

streets, pretending it were one of time's carats,
making claims not worth a tinker's cuss, but
smiling as if all work were illustrious. I'm sick

of the moon whose far side no gold can limn,
of the brass sales of my neighbours' shops,
of tipping dreams into bargains and watching

the stars sharpen to jewels in the ear-pins
of usurers, smoothing a look in the demoted
lustre of my pots. But I'll go on – no matter

how the world glints my loss, or the spokes
of my wheels mint out their counterfeit suns;
life declassed of its sheen. I'll just spruik up

my mock brilliance, prink up another day
in the dull patina of my pots, and call out *iron,*
scraps – as if I could believe in my own finesse.

The Lake

At dusk she walks to the lake. On shore
a few egrets are pinpointing themselves
in the mud. Swallows gather the insect lint

off the velvet reed-heads and fly up through
the drapery of willows. It is still hot.
Those clouds look like drawn-out lengths

of wool untwilled by clippers. The egrets
are poised now – moons just off the wane –
and she thinks, too, how their necks are

curved like fingernails held out for manicure.
She walks the track that's a draft of the lake
and gazes at where light nurses the wounded

capillaries of a scribbly gum. A heron on one leg
has the settled look of a compass, though soon,
in flight, it will have the gracility of silk

when it's wound away. She has always loved
the walks here, the egrets stepping from
the lute music of their composure, the mallards

shaking their tails into the chiffon wakes,
the herons fletching their beaks with moths
or grasshoppers, the ibis scything the rushes

or poking at their ash-soft tail feathers.
Soon the pelicans will sail in, fill and filter
the pink. Far off, she can see where tannin

has seeped from the melaleucas, a burgundy
stain slow as her days spent among tiles and
Formica. She's glad now she's watching water

shift into the orange-tipped branches of a
she-oak, a wren flick its notes towards the wand
of another's twitching tail. There's an oriole

trilling at the sun, a coveted berry, a few
cicadas still rattling their castanets. She loves
those casuarinas, far-off, combed and groomed,

trailing their branches: a troupe of orang-utans
with all that loping, russet hair; and when
the wind gets into them, there's a sound as if

seeds were being sorted, or feet shuffled among
the quiet gusts of maracas. Soon the lights
on the opposite shore will come on *like little*

electric fig seeds and she will walk back
listening to frogs croak in the rushes, the bush
fill with the slow cisterns of crickets, her head

with the quiet amplitude of – Keats perhaps,
or a breeze consigning ripples to the bank;
the sun, an emblazoned lifebuoy, still afloat.

Woman and Child

They listen to the myna birds dicker in the grass.
        The child's blue shoes are caked with
garden dirt. When he runs, she sees the antics
        of a pair of wrens. She works the garden,

a pot of rusting gardenias has given off its ales
        and infused the danker germinations of her
grief. She watches her son chase pigeons,
        kick at the leaves piled high. Now, a magpie

adds to his cascades of laughter as he runs with
        the hose, pours a fine spray, happy to be giving
to the grass this silver courtship. She sighs,
        watches the drops settle in. Today, who

can explain the sadness she feels. Surely this
        day is to be treasured: the sun out, the breeze
like a cat's tongue licking a moon of milk;
        her son expending himself in small, public

bursts, happy among clover where bees hover,
        and unfold centrefolds of nectar. Today,
who can explain the heaviness in her head, as if
        all her worries were tomes toward a larger work,

one she knows she will never finish, but to which
	she must keep adding, thought by thought.
She sweeps the petals, smells their russet imprint.
	Soon dusk will come with an envoy of smoke

and her son outlast her patience by a rose.
	Already he is tiring, pulling at the flowers.
It won't be long before they'll go in, listen
	to the jug purr comfort. He'll sleep and she'll

lie back, or get up to unhook the cry of her cat
	from the wire door. Now a few cicadas are idling,
giving each other the gun, and a cockatoo calls,
	a haughty felon. She sighs, knowing she won't

escape her mood today, the turned earth
	or its rank persuasions; her child's petulance
flaring like an orchid, or a cockatoo's unruly crest.
	Today, she knows she will need to consider

her unhappiness, of what she is a prisoner – if not
	the loss of hope's particulars. Her son soaks
the path, rinses the sky of its featureless blue.
	He is giving that water, now, to everything.

Whisky Grass

Only this morning I felt anxiety's tufted leaves,
and with no scythe or sickle, I put my lips
to a common roadside weed, survivor in poorly
drained soils, and blew: my tongue feeling
for the strange venation, the mid-rib ligule fringed
with hairs, until it returned the sting of whisky grass
and the taste of brown flowers. Over and over
the same note matting itself into the ground.
So many reasons to be torn, pressed down
to the seeping wound, or the salve. So many reasons
why beauty can't square up all people in this world
and give them the insouciance of flowers.
All morning my mind gone to seed in margins,
waste places, held back by understoreys of wire
and the milky latex of plants no one would give
their cold acres for. So many reasons
raising themselves to the repeating power
of our mouths. We pull all kinds of things
out of the ground; we cut off what we can
and paint it clean. We let birds pull songs through
hedge-work whose tidiness we can't attend to,
let alone afford. Beauty likes its borders green.
So many reasons why these whiskered shoots
claim my mind, and why nothing looks greener
against the rain. Sure, these leaves by nightfall

might be shredded by birds foraging among dirt
dumped over yellow, defoliated stems; the sap taken
by dreams, as every rhizome is raked from the ground.
I work a tune around a crowning blade and let it
loosen another runner, testing the future. The wild
may never give up its gestures. Not while beauty
poises itself on the edge, trying to name the place
it's native to; a tongue twisting round each
bearded stalk, listening from the understorey
for a flute-like sound, so many reasons
staking their season again. All morning anxiety's
notes pour through head-high grass. The sky
turns and turns – a shiver of exhausted leaves,
perpetuals that always seem to come too soon.

The Fisherman's Son

Perhaps it was when he first felt his shoulders
roll an oar, or when he pulled the thick boots on.
Perhaps it was when he saw the curved thin rod
of the moon angle into his father's face and hook
his mouth into an ugly grin; or when the sun
rerouted his eyes to the necks of wading birds
along the shore, as the first pink tones of dusk

uncurled along the ferns. It could have been
the way his father's knife eased out the eyes of so
many fish like spoonfuls of compote that gave
him thoughts black as the inky emulsions of squid,
a sleep no fishing boat could ease, nor star prick
with its comforting pin. Perhaps he learned nothing
from his father's face, except how whisky

trawled sleep from his eyes and left him pursued
by pain and thunder and a show of lightning's
yellow flares. Perhaps it was when he felt the rod
pull his arms through a reel's band of static;
when he heard his father's voice in the headache
scudding low across his forehead, the reel
with an insect's drumhead pitch his heart into

summer's mounting heat; the slow drip of days
revved up by outboards then dispelled by a drill
of mosquitoes, or weather finding tenor in its squalls.
Among stars and fish, those notes from the waste
hours he gutted, from the river's sweep of years,
who could know how many knives he heard
audition his nerves, or what beat his heart

took; or how many rounds of an ingoing lake
before the wind rushed into the uncaulked
cracks and left him face down, deep-drummed,
gear-slipped, deaf to his inner repertoire, blind
now to the river's weather-beaten stare.
Perhaps from a tangle of yellow air, or when
he heard the wind bale out of a speeding sky,

or a firetail add its flute to the rankling handle
of a windlass, a lyrebird weigh its call in
with an anchor's unrolling links, some twisting
erratic pull of tackle as the mosquitoes buzzed;
when he heard his father's voice in each dizzy
injected dose... All day such talk went on
as the men brought in their hauls, gutting fish

to the noise of pelicans, those bills clacking
like clapperboards, the ease of routine. Here
among the brace of tides, as wind skips along
ropes left lank and loose and dangling now
among the sloops, no one fully knowing why
a boy would desire to die… The avocets walking
the shore with their hesitant, hair-splitting steps.

Wolf Notes

I

This is the place the dogs are sent
to reconnoitre. This is the place
the dogs are sent to reconnoitre.
This is the place, this is the place
I've ached for, pulled the chain
of a long tendon and ached for.

All summer dreaming of the haste
of hounds. All summer dreaming
the leg remembers, remembers
the pain it was chained for, running
with the whelps. This is the place
where the chain broke, pulling

against pain. This is the place
of the thin, distal nail; of a moon
buried in the teeth of the pack;
of a claw broken off in the lock,
when I stretched and ached and
like prey, pulled myself down.

This is the place, this is the place
I'm a cur for, my mouth the wound
of a cruel ground. But this place
is beyond knowing. This is the place

all dogs are sent to reconnoitre,
beyond the necessities of war.

2

Go on: try to change the place
that's fathered by the metallic nail
of a single howl. Try the fence
line, the dingos foreign to it,
able to take the taste of stones.
Already stars menace the hills

with fixed arrivals, and the moon
that keeps the darkness out
with its cold arson, lights up
the folds in the dingo's ear
carrying the circumcision stones.
Men talk on faintly lit graves

when the sky slits itself open
to the drawn-out terror of sirens.
Go on: the sky has already put
down its mark, and before we'll
seek the water that will soak
the blood from the ground,

we wait behind grey stones.
In our hearts, poison and black
wulfenite in a strangled moan.

Look, all our lives we've been
baiting the wrong animal,
unable to stop because they know.

3

The moon hung like a dewclaw.
Sirius lay dogged. Even the sun
was terrierised: so far off, so beaten
back. I walked into a wind where
winter's forty-two teeth were bared
covering everything with a jackal's

breath. I felt yellow eyes signal
to a pack. In the dunged-out dark
I was mongrelised by the boned
apparition of my own face. Yes,
I was doggerelled, kennelled-out
over-whelped. So many dogmas,

doggeries and the vulpine crimes
of the past. I longed for elephants,
tigers, for a leopard's or a viper's
stealth. Then, I listened deep
from the pit of the dog-watch,
from my mind's cold lair, from

foxglove, hound's tongue and from
a field of sweet, dog-eared trees –
and heard how the wolf notes
show up on the dogvane, are borne
by the strength of the dogwood,
are healed by the wolf's bane.

An Artist Speaks to his Model

What can I ask of your lips
that they haven't already given
my colourless signature; of your
hands other than to shade
your eyes as the sun burnishes
the windows, then carries on
to the grey porticos of the square.
I see pigeons on the gold-lit roof
of the Cathedral of St Christopher,
and as I stir my brush about
my palette – scarlet is what
I pray for; scarlet that flows under
a vanquished bridge; that lives
with finches in the tops of trees
because, desire, you said,
should always live on the wing.
As I hold my brush, your skin
is a breaking wound. I could
mend it with all the things
I know I'll one day lose, but
now I imagine you're only one
red facade away from my slender
stairwell, lindens and chestnuts
dropping their blossoms onto
the street. Elise, I know you live
by endless esplanades, by fierce

pigments, by the rich gilt with
which you shine your dreams
into the colour of absent things,
but we belong to rooms, Elise,
whose heat prompts curtains
to blow, and the skin to seek
communion with the blue-black
night. Sometimes I don't know
what is memory, what dream.
Last night through the slant beat
of the rain, I thought I saw you
leaning against an easeled arch,
a vertigo of colour sweeping
your face. Elise, my heart is
placed before the marble steps
I would have you reach, but
I know nothing can capture you.
Perhaps only the muted leaf
the wind takes. I search all
the shades the wind might bruise
you with, days in these bitten-out
streets. Impossible to get your
lips to resemble fate. Soon,
the pine limbs will disorder
my yard, the load of needles
shake loose, and the finches
peck at seed dropped by women
whose hands – dark, serene –

tend an earth whose lilacs are close.
Elise, around your shoulders
I'll paint blood. Around your
breasts an expedience of leaves.
I'm waiting for the light to be
cornered on the sill. I'm waiting
for your voice to short out
my heart along the quickly burning
length of St Christopher's spire.
Already an unthankful moon
has climbed opposite the sun.

The Courtesan

1

Dark was just coming on. Lightning flexed
its muscled whip. The rain fell in heavy drops.
Steadily, the clouds puffed up. Many times

I thought I knew the predicted outcome.
I thought I knew the way the evening would
turn out, sure and tight – a monkey's tail-ring.

2

These ascetics with their vainglorious celibacy.
They come to my door with their alms bowls.
At first they have downcast eyes. I like to

play a game: I fill their bowls not with food –
but with water's mirror. When they see
my face reflected, then they thirst. And,

as I turn to go, they beckon me, sated by
so much sun, begging me to stay, before
some icy penitence reseeds their ground.

3

Today, the fishmonger comes with his vanilla
scented breath. How shall I bear him, slippery
as water? I laugh at him and his vinegar eels.

And later, the gaze of that poppy seed seller
will work itself into my clothes. At least
he's better than the thistle-lopper, whose eyes

latch onto my skin like beggar's ticks, or lice
sewn down without tenderness. Afterwards,
I prickle and smart, then feel numb for hours.

4

Who he was I couldn't say. Not the usual man
who wants to be worked with casually: his
routine hardness placed in your working hand.

O, how I'll remember him under the weight
of the millstone maker, the grain sack puller,
the mausoleum attendant with his callous breath.

Even under the pulverising weight of the mortar
and pestle maker, who comes to me cold and
anxious – hoping I'll make easier work of his son.

5

I once thought this life to be good as any other.
I'd look up at the sky and assess the weather:
at least there'd be those rain squalls of luxury.

Now, only empty-handed sky, and tufts
of thin, disappearing cloud… O, how I still look
for thunderbolts in the silk-unraveller's hands.

6

No matter how hard I clung I felt the tip
of lightning extinguish my hold. I felt the wind
push. For the first time I felt my body slip,

I felt thunder scud… Then, suddenly I felt
cold, utterly mizzled on. I felt the doldrums
blacken the eye of the storm… Then,

I began staring out into long snowdrifts –
as if I'd become a woman who can command
a season to leave when she narrows her fan.

7

Here, moodily watching my scarlet carp.
Sometimes, a band of sunlight strikes and I can
see into their dark insides. They flit quickly

about the knife-edge light, as the eyes of these
men do, trying to pare away my smile, the one
I paint on with red. But they know the shape

my tongue has in the thick green depths.
And I know the taste of them, pressed into
me bitter as weed, over which these waters pass.

8

He loved best my aviary. He'd spend hours
teaching those parrots songs and palindromes.
One day when a pangolin got into the bantams

he composed a most beautiful dirge. Strangest
man, happiest among birds. All he wanted
of me was to recline each evening on a bed

of owl and linnet feathers. Later, he developed
a passion for oriental fowl. I began to feel
outclassed by the guinea hens. So I dismissed

him, regretting it a little… I still miss the way
he'd speak to those parrots, teaching them his
sonnets and how to repeat them backwards.

9

Poetry, never one of my accomplishments,
came to me one day in the yard. I can no better
explain it than I can the wind blowing its bell-like

scales into these chimes. I can't remember what
I composed, only that my voice seemed to turn
into a wind-crafted charm... I think of it on dull

afternoons, abstractedly reciting from a canon
of ghazals to some pewter-maker's ignorant sons.
I hope for a glint, some further crystalline tune

to turn my tongue away from this routine tang,
from these faces, which, on hearing anything near
to poetry, turn the separate greys of lead and tin.

10

When I'm feeling desolate, I recite the names
of winds: *haboob, sirocco, zonda, simoon.*
Sometimes, when unkind hands take me in

to their whirlwinds, I say: *saistan, dust storm,*
mistral, typhoon. I don't know why, but in
these atmospheres of power and guilt, I try

to look into the eye-wall of the hurricane and
shout out to the forces of deflection. I'm sick
of my words evaporating into pale skies and

into the false dawns of blandishment. I'll wait
for the monsoon-predictor, his head always
true, and homing in like a pilot balloon.

At Dusk

The lightning gets busy this side
of silence, and when the moon
appears from among a few wind-nicked
clouds, she will hear the crows
as they fly westwards like the dark
debris of the fruit bats testing every threshold.
The earth is not yet a bell ringing
for the lost, only what's left
under the boards of the porch that take
the heavily repeated riffs of a guitar, Janis
Joplin haemorrhaging through a hi-fi.
Smoke from her cigarette
is coiling close to the faint sheen of her lips.
Static sizzles, and there's the sound of a zapper
short-circuiting the lives of moths
and midges, though she thinks
only of the soundless storms of love
her lips are giving lyrics to. Noise, quiet as
it is kept, is not what she wants of the dusk,
but she turns up the sound,
and plays to the thunder. She rocks
and hums, and her voice is the shadowy
foliage where spiders live, suspended
in time. She thinks how she
yields each night to the assassin bug's

blue spit; everything saying she needs Joplin's
flyblown whine, cicadas holding
the pedal down. Inside,
there's nothing but husks, dry leaves
blowing towards the back of her life, drumfire
igniting like a headache. Two fence posts
away, a cat defines with its wail
one point of speech. Insects are still
building their head of steam. She can hear
traffic's burr, feel the tap of her pulse
like a trapped ghost,
feel longing string height to her blood,
an implacable gnat, a bug that never
lets up. Soon the muddy voices will
ooze back, guitars that licked
the air with hottest lightning, wait once
more. Then she'll hear the crickets start up
in the earth, and she'll sit with herself
in the dark, listening to the rain
fall across the path, to mosquitoes etch
long cries, before a stylus winds its way
inwards again, and she hangs in its
tight web, safe with what she hears.

Storm and Honey

The Shark

We heard the creaking clutch of the crank
as they drew it up by cable and wheel
and hung it sleek as a hull from the roof.

Grennan jammed open the great jaws
and we saw how the upper jaw hung from
the skull. We flinched at the stench of blood

that dripped on the fishhouse floor, and
even Davey – when Grennan reached in
past the scowl and the steel prop for the

stump – just about passed out. The limb's
skin had already blanched, a sight none
of us could stomach, and we retched,

though Grennan, cool, began cutting off
the flesh in knots, slashing off the flesh
in strips; and then Davey, flensing and

flanching, opened up the stomach and
the steaming bowels. Gulls circled like
ghouls. Still they taunt us with their cries

and our hearts still burn inside us when
we remember, how Grennan with a tool
took out what was left of the child.

The Cast

I flick out my line, it's pale and thin as the antennae
of the crayfish probing over the rim of the bucket.
I can hear them scrabble, their heavy claws trying to grip
the metal sides. Grennan throws a rock at the bucket,

the crayfish settle, but then their feelers pick around
the rim again as if trying to assess what's keeping them
in this cold, curved place. Grennan casts out, a long
tearing sound. 'One good cast will take you right

to where the fish prick the surface,' he says, and covers
another hook with a new section of prawn. Davey
is still turning over his reel, clicking it, calibrating,
counting as though he were sure he could crack that pack

of digits, or break into the structure of brute matter itself.
Grennan's next line goes taut, mine's still slack. Davey
still doesn't cast, he just turns and tests his tackle,
he watches Grennan and me, listens to our reels, to his own

as he revolves it, cracks it, working at its precision,
desperately waiting for it to click part of himself into being.
We say nothing to one another, but listen hard to those claws
clutching at the sides of the bucket, trying to catch the rim.

Spittle Beach

It's cold among the shiftings of shell and sand;
the rain falling slantwise out at sea. I walk among the pylons,
fish-scales are stuck to the wood like grey sleet.
Far-off, a yacht –

its spinnaker filled with the wind looks as bulbous
as the vocal sac of a bell toad or a bullfrog. Along the shore
weed, and the blunt white shells of cuttlefish;
jellyfish like smeared

globs of glyceride. An octopus, its head like a perfume
bottle's puffer, has just squirted a whift of ink, tentacles
curl in the air like baby fingers while the man hauls it in.
Yesterday there was a shoal

of fish turning through the current like a mirror-ball,
or like a cluster of silver birch leaves in a swirling wind.
Now just the weed rolling in, dark shadows from the deep.
I walk and feel the wind

come off the full fetch of the bay. Men in the distance
are flicking lines out, they are spectred by the spume;
even the rocks and headland seem ghost-dreamt.
Soon more of the wave-peaked sea

will reach inwards, breakers give off more spindrift.
I walk towards the rock pools full of shells, hermit crabs,
and lilac anemones. Another octopus rapidly opens
and closes, a spanning

spinning hand. Near the boathouse is a washed-up skate,
a boy lifts it above his head – he's a waiter with a drinks tray –
then he hurls it hard, back to the sea. It whidders down
as quietly as a UFO.

I walk back where the bluebottles are cast up in clusters
of varicose knots, and where the moon appears to be
a squid fisherman's underwater, halogen light
trying to burn through.

Inlet

The lighthouse beam swings round again, lighting
	the sea up all the way to the horizon.
Nothing is broken yet by rain, by birds collapsing
	their wings as they fall. Already
the sun has tired, losing stroke. I dangle a line,

feel a few bites shuttle up and down the nylon.
	Soon I'll see the moon over
the bluff, a spike wound with pale gauze, stars
	spawning in the breaking swells
that leak over the oars. Now a heron, air-built,

takes off on silent hinges and little currents swirl
	around my prow as I work my arms
backwards, forwards, my oars like whispering
	shuttles lifting the water into
fine-spun thread. Everything will change, I know:

a heavy curtain of rain come, the moon slip away
	as I draw harder on the oars.
I know my stroke will lose rhythm in the brown
	waters of the cove, but now I make
curved passage across the bay where even Grennan

or Davey on the far-off jetty, their reels spinning
like a sudden volley of insects
cued by the dusk, might, just possibly – when
they come into the presence
of still waters – find something beautiful to say.

Tackle

'I love the heavy crackle of an old '50s spinner,'
Davey says, pointing to an antique Bakelite reel. 'That one
was made by a dentist, or a locksmith –
I can't remember, but it's a good clacker, you'd think
you heard a clinker drop anchor at Rickets pier.'

Just then rain ticks on the wheelhouse roof
as though Kalahari tribesmen had gathered, all chatting
in their clicking dialects. Davey, oblivious,
continues, 'I like a reel to sound as if it ground shell grit.
I like it to bitch-box its hisses, I like the full

clack and brattle and not just have it chitter
like a sorry crab.' Then he spits phlegm onto the deck,
points out his favourite – a zinc Bakelite
antique with an adjustable crank and wishbone brake –
made, he claims, by a machinist who built parts

for the Bomb. 'Listen to that,' he says, giving
the reel a few turns. Grennan says it sounds like gamma
ray flak, that perhaps its maker left
in parts meant for the Bomb. I say it's no different from
the rain, or a vat of Davey's home brew when

it starts to spume and scum. Davey spits again,
turns back to work on a rusted engine bit; then in the same
gruff register of a motor he's been revving
above the rain, Grennan says, 'Listen to this,' and gases
the engine again, 'better than a burst of cranky

surf running crab-wise up sand.' Davey spins
a metal mooching reel whose sizzle seems to climb all the way
to the hot tin roof. Turning towards them
and trying not to sound alarmed, 'That whirler there,' I say
pointing to the storm, 'isn't that what we ought

to be reckoning with?' Thunder drums its set
of slag-hacking hammers, clouds discharge yellow
like a ruck of panicking cuttlefish.
Just then our boat lunges. I look towards the bluff
and see the lighthouse glow sharp, neat, and clean,

'A whale's tooth,' I say, 'etched by the scrimshawing
lightning,' but no one laughs, or gives the storm a look.
Davey spins a graphite reel with machine-cut gears
and a locomotive level-wind. Joking, Grennan says,
'It's just a cicada croaking in the throat of a bird.'

At the Bay

I've been reeling in my line and casting out, listening
to the waves rap the shells along the shore like a jingle-fitted drum,
but I've caught nothing. I think I'd better go back to the boat
and just watch shore birds slowly step; perhaps watch

them beat unhurried spondees over the rushes when they fly
towards home. I see the breezes shirr and gather at the water's
edge where the shoals fold over and over; it makes me
want to stay and cast again, and keep in earshot the crests

that cap and crash quietly with the dusk; to stay and watch
if fish will flash their fire; hear my reel play itself the way
an insect clicks its beats in maddening heat. But today
I may not catch a single fish. Perhaps better just to turn

away, watch the egret put its icy steps along the sand; turn
and step away, let my rod bear each question lightly as I see
the egret flex its feet; step and turn away, content if these
waters hold only reflection, content if they do, or do not tremble.

Delancey

He lived in a shack on Bennetts Creek.
The mudflats were black and always stank;
he said it was because they were full
of bacteria that stripped the oxygen
from the sulphate compounds and gave
off toxic gas, but it was a beautiful place.
The crabs would come out onto the silt
at low tide and feed like a regiment.
You could hear the flacker of the ducks
as they took off through the mangroves,
those roots you thought might almost
begin to smoke. We'd sit and watch
the crabs, or mend some nets, or he'd rub
away at a spark plug yellow as a dugong's
tooth, or we'd watch the stars come on
close as town lights. I liked his manner,
the way his expression would inexplicably
change, the way he'd turn his head this
way and that as though before he spoke
he was trying each thought like a key.
He told me once he thought the moon
was as beautiful as a find of Turkish
meerschaum. Eventually he left. Kids
burnt down his shack one night, stalking
the derelict track. We saw those flames
from as far away as the wharf. I never

went back to the creek, but I think
often of how we'd listen to the crabs
sucking out their Morse from the mud.
I can still see him walking across
the marsh flats, fervently stropping
his hands through a mist of mosquitos
and gnats to reach me and our spot
by the fallen logs. Delancey had told me
that the creek wasn't the place to get
answers, but that it would give me
questions as fine as the sediment burrowed
from the mud by the yabbies and crabs.
Sometimes I catch myself shaking
my head the way he did, just working
it slowly like a sieve at the water's edge.

Jellyfish

Jellyfish translucent as onionskin pulse through the bay.
Davey gets one on his oar and lifts it up like a dripping wad

of plastic wrap. I see others floating in and out of the shallows,
changing colour like globes of thin photosensitive glass.

Later when they're washed up like old bait bags, kids
will pierce them with sticks. At least today the onshore wind

isn't driving those bluebottles in. Yesterday we scooped
up some with our oars and burst their gas-filled floats.

Grennan became angry. He told us a bluebottle was not
a single animal, but a specialised colony. Then he dangled

one of the long fishing tentacles from his rod, it was as ragged
as a skein of unpicked knitting. Davey said later he thought

he was going to lash us with it, especially when the veins
in his neck and forehead turned blue and knotted. Davey

lowers the jellyfish back into the bay – a quivering mound.
I think we can still see Grennan's face and neck, the bulging

circuitry of veins; still feel his mouth venting words with about
as much sour air as we'd burst from those gas-filled floats.

At 5am

Grennan sucks in air along his gums and yells again
    to Davey who is filling the trough
of the gunwale with scrabbling crabs. Lightning
    slips down the sky like a forkful
of buttered seaworms. The rain works fast, cutting

with decisive precision across the sea. Grennan
    pulls in squid then severs the slimy
cordage of the tentacles, throws one at Davey
    who laughs, his voice hard, sharp
as a scuttling tool. I bring up more pots as wind

rattles the uneven links that my palms pay in
    before I let down the crash
of another stone-weighted creel. My heart drums
    as I pull in the loads. My stomach
rumbles, turns like a captured ghost as the boat

rides a thick swell. The crabs that are in the hold
    are going claw to claw, outdoing
the clatter of the hail that falls across the deck
    like marble scree. Squid ink roils
across the deck oily as a thunderhead. Grennan

pierces the squid's eye with the end of a blade,
    soft fruit he'll save later for
pelicans when their beaks clash in the quieter air.
    Each day we go out among
the slippery stench of weather's trouble to work

like sea bulls in the rain's surge and swell. Each day
    we follow lightning's flickering
pulse, the black slough when clouds flume their
    tempests. We see squid turn
orange, red, green in a spectrum of unearthly dawns.

Grennan throws a squid's eye and another tentacle
    at Davey who has just tied
a crab's pincer into a crescent moon. He laughs,
    rain spatters against his fingers,
the ink like thick rope winding down his arms.

A Shanty

Old Man Seiner lets the lines
go out past shells that rattle
across dark, nautical floors.
Old Man Seiner hears blood
in the blue-lit corridors, then paces
the sea with a zinc-steel sun.

Old Man Seiner makes a shore
then sheathes his needles.
He holds his net to deck
the trawlers free of whispers.
He works each thread
clear of the limpet tempers

of the sailors who drop
each net, then sit for hours
in bottled depths to talk
of what the shadow-foulers do
to crews of windblown yachts.
Old Man Seiner floats

his wrack. He knows that by
the lilting tinkle of a boat
at anchor, or by the fish
that drift between a cork
and sinker, through all
the uncaulked cracks he'll

keep his shuttle back.
Old Man Seiner works
the docks, casts his gill-slit eyes
to narrow depths. He knows
how his horizons bear
his yachts, in candle mass,

and how the heron's flight
can put a weighted cadence
on the tongues of men whose
hook-snared fingers fray
old rope, whose eyes enlist
the lights of devilfish.

He brings his shuttle back
across the mist, across the weed
to trail his angling sight,
across the windblown
offshore wave-crests
breaking into starry nights.

Gale

I vomit across the tiller, gunwale and deck
        dumping more than a monsoon
would into the Bay of Bengal. One more load
        I think and I might change
the entire hydrological cycle of our small inlet.

With every lurch of our boat I stagger, trying
        to wear this gale like a fisherman's
sweater. Then a scuttling wave comes and I hold
        my footing in half a metre
of deck swill before it gushes out of the scuppers.

Already Grennan has peeled the steel swivels
        off the leader cart, stuck squid
onto the hooks, fixed the swivels onto the mainline
        and thrown the lot over the side.
Davey has locked a ball-drop on a line, checked

where the mainline has snagged spooling off
        the big drum. My stomach
feels as though it were being keelhauled,
        my head as though it were
jammed into a set of isometric pressure lines

going into a cyclonic spin. When I vomit again
    Davey says I look as ugly
and expendable as a bucket of badly iced brill.
    Then my feet slip from under me
and I'm carried along by the moshing swill.

Rain is falling so fast it looks as if fishmongers
    are scaling the day's catch.
I hear my breath repeating a calamity like the sea's.
    Over my shoulder I can see
the lightning trip wildly, a venom-transmitting

nerve. Then it jolts rapidly across the sky again
    streamlining out like a frog's
electrode-prodded legs. Another wave crashes in.
    A rod slopes, bends. Grennan
grabs it, crosscutting boldly the italicising wind.

Grennan Mending Nets

So good to sit and work, taking thread
from warp to weft; to listen to the sea
pull in and out without a thought for tarry

or departure, even for what the boats
have caught. His fingers work the mesh,
the open weave, twisting, until it seems

the sea itself is locked. He works at dusk.
He sees the shallows give the mulloway
back and how a veil of shadowed light

falls across the inlet's inwrought gold,
its wide-armed shore. Soon he'll portion
out his stories of harbour and shipwreck,

or blow into his flagon like a clarinet.
He likes to watch the albatross, to listen
to the boatmen haul their ropes in a swirl

of onshore breeze, to watch a windlass
raise an anchor up. He likes to tell his stories,
to bring his shuttle up and, in rhythm

with the yachts, to tie his knots. Already
the light has pulled away from boats
we may never see again, and though his hands

hold weight, he likes to let his mind drift,
then let it find its place, a cut and finished
thread at the back of the tatted shore.

Octopus

I look up towards the headland at the lighthouse.
        Frigate hawks are blowing down in dusky
scraps. In the distance I can hear a blowhole

throwing the spray of a shattered wave into the air,
        the sea hissing like a bandwidth of mistuned
frequencies. I climb towards the headland, sand

stings my legs as if a volley of pins were being spat
        from a peashooter. The tide with its smell of
salt and dreck is already receding. When I reach

the headland I stand and watch gannets fight
        for purchase on the lighthouse that looks
for a moment like a statue of a headless pope.

Not long ago I'd dropped a whole load of cod,
        brill and black skimmer bream down
the gap between the pier and the hull. Already

I think I can hear Grennan's voice in grey salt,
        threshing in the shallows, addressing the flies,
myself and the sea-lice in a tone only a ruined

and ruthless fishermen would weigh in from
    a raw and unforgiving sea. I sit for a while
in the spume of the salt until the wind like a taut

rope holds me. When I come down the wind
    has dropped, bluebottles are washing up
on the sand. It is quieter now, only the waves

roaring then flattening into a monotone as grim
    as the rumble of a carburettor living on
poor gas. In the west clouds are hanging oddly

above the range, cast-iron blocks whose hoist
    chains might snap; rain is fretting again
from the gouty end of the sky. Ahead on the pier

I can see Grennan hauling up an octopus, its arms
    flailing about the way rubber does when it's
stripping off a blowing tyre. Some ink shoots out

like dark hot propellant just as he gets his knife
    into it... I feel suddenly cold... cold
as something laid out on a fishmonger's slab.

Joe

One day in high summer, a fire swept all the way down
from Woodman's Point; river cruise patrons were lunching –
beer, prawns and 40s band music – at a posh place called
Nudibranchs. When firemen arrived the place was already
falling into the river; smoking beams and balustrades, black
stink of ash for weeks. The cruises would run all the way
up to Waterfall Point, one of the best spots on the river
with rushes, willows and freckled ducks. Grennan used
to bring the prawns up to the restaurant where he'd have
a few pints with Joe, the cruise operator. They'd talk
and watch the light arrive in splashes on the river.
The day the fire came you could see the flames all the way
back to the inlet. The fire took twelve lives. After that Joe
became a wreck of man, stranded on an edgeless waste
of himself, ghost-written by smoke. Grennan would see him
down at the pier, throwing in a line then straight away
pulling it back, talking incessantly to himself. Then he'd
stagger off, caught always in his own whirlpool, an awful
wash spinning him round. Some nights he'd be swigging
from an old bailing can, yelling into the spindrift. He would
hold his head in his hands and see smoke fill his head again
as he listed back and forth, retching, coughing as though
the air, after all this time, was still lacking anything
to breathe. Some of us tried to help him get back on his feet,
help him run his cruises again, but his boats just rusted
alongside disused barges and ore boats in slicks of oil

and diesel, and though every day his head would burn
it was unable to burn free... Grennan found him up near
the oyster leases, one side of him buried in the mud,
the other infested with caddis flies and soldier crabs
whose carapaces were the bright blue of high-summer skies.
He seemed almost peaceful, Grennan had told us later,
grief slipping in the liquid ruin of all the whisky he'd
been drinking as he told us again of the times he'd sound
three blasts for Joe to shunt the boom open where
the river would pull and splash by the dock, how they'd
sit with amber drinks in the amber weather and discuss
his plans to make *Nudibranchs* the best place on the river.
We all fell silent following our thoughts back again
through the summer air to the willows, to the afternoon
breezes getting up, to the sound of ducks moving through
the reeds, to the band music audible across the river.

River Music

The mouth of a little fish had just sipped away a star
from the river, a lyrebird was opening the day, volunteering
to be a bell. We were watching an egret prod at the nutrient
dark, its beak one tine of a fork catching what floats, just
as the sun began cracking the trees awake. The bird's song

reached us, then it sharded into the river's cold glass.
You thought you heard it again in the eddying backwash.
A frog began to ratchet, self-correcting like a clock. Our
boat swung away on the revolutions of its propeller, water
adjusted its slap, displacing sound in the cutaway rock

and then the egret stepped into a sun-shaft; a crow flew
down, made its slain-in-the-spirit human sound. Cicadas
drummed hard against a sky turning cold, vitrified. Wind
came, then the rain. Then the wind dropped into the reeds,
though you said it was the bird again and its sly alarm.

We found hooks enough to load our lines, let our reels
click the hours away with the quick flicking of our casts.
I heard a bird fly into the pin oaks, the swamp gums, then
into the tupelos with barely a sound. All the way home
I turned the oars hard, making a round music with my arms.

Morning, Upriver

At times you can hear the slow seep of the gases, or
the sweet decomposing twitter of a scrub wren, or a mopoke's
two notes pumping like an oar-beat across the bay. If you
wait you can see the quarter moon break through the mist,

or through cool, interleaving rain. You wouldn't think
it would be beautiful in the cold, scratched light; insects
circling before they set off towards a day's smear of blood.
I come here often, sometimes just to listen to the chug

of a punt, or to see a swamp harrier land on a sagging branch.
Sometimes a chat will fly low into the reeds, or an egret
step high among the eelgrass before it shifts its reflection
into the shallows, or across the side-sliding slosh of a ripple.

When the mist lifts I wait for king parrots to call bright as this
river's glint, as the light in a flooded gum. I row into the shadows
of a saltwater paperbark as branches stir the brackish wash.
I think of my trip back down – and I rock in my silver skiff.

Capricorn

Through the end of an old Coke bottle he tracks
    the flight of a petrel until it is tattered by
sea-wind and another blurred mintage of the sun.
    Along the pier he hears the men with their
reels, with their currency of damp sand. His rod
    quivers, weighted not with fish, but with

the names of storms: *Harmattan, Vendavales,*
    turbid winds running the vanguard of
dangerous straits. He kicks at a pile of fish scales,
    galleon ballast, a hoard of ducats spilled
from an old Dutch dogger. The men will soon
    chase him off, this raucous hero plundering

brigs. But now the bottle is a horn into which
    he pours so much breath; and the air has
a tone borrowed from a blowhole, from wind
    singing through a bridge's rusting struts.
A crab sifts sand grains for its hole. Its claw,
    an old sea-brigand's hook, is paying out

doubloons and threats. Ah, but you know, if
    you were to take this child's hand; if you
were to keep his gaze in yours and wait for
    each circulation of his breath; if you were

to watch the pirated scenes of daydreams
        play out through a windfall of glass, then

you'd see the copper-coloured sun. You'd walk
        this beach a long time with your thoughts
trading in weather and wind, the petrels keeping
        pace with the rakish lines of dreams
sailing in with the clinker-built storms. The past
        and the present would not be depressions

facing each other, nor would there be grains
        of sand abrading your fate. On the shore
a gull, dead from the night's storm. With his rod
        the boy flings it up, the glove of a dueller
he's just Zorroed with his sword. No, the world
        would not be a wave repeating its collapse,

but whatever mintage of story a boy can find
        among fish scales, sand and the common
issuance of wind; a boy who knows nothing
        of the linkages between storms; nor of
the men, yet, who log weather's quick decay
        onto gauges of abuse; who knows nothing
about paying for that old voyage toward death.

Rain

Rain bubble-wrapping the windows. Rain
falling as though someone ran a blade down the spines
of fish setting those tiny backbones free. Rain
with its squinting glance, rain

with its rustle of descending silk. Rain, rain,
the cascading rain outrunning its own skeins in the lilting
dark. The loquacious rain, glissading across
the drip-garrulous leaves. Tipsy

rain, puddling, wetting its own socks. Rain's
swirl at my feet smelling of leaf musk. Rain falling
like seed-gobs in the streetlight's tumbledown gloom.
Sifted rain, purling, paying

its way while its veil makes a thin distance.
Rain spiccatoing over wavelets and their hilly crests.
Rain cashing up along the skyline of gold-minted lights.
Rain nibbling at the grass

with broken teeth. Crestfallen rain leaving
the road, then riffling through the lop-eared treetops.
Rain tangle-footed, half out of its clothes. Sweeps
of rain like hair,

like pampas stalks, wind-tarried, bending; or tall,
ornamental, moving louchely and skew-whiff. Rain's
drops when they begin to fly as though they're being
shuddered off

a shaggy dog. Rain wayworn in the slippery
night, drumbling across awnings, gutters, windows, walls
and slowing down those tittupy drops until the sky
like a new god glozes

with a little rollicking thunder and lets the first
light through in luteous gloops. But then more rain, more
clouds stacking up, rain that will come down fast
again, like grain from gunnysacks.

Appaloosa

I have always loved the word guitar

DAVID ST. JOHN

I have never been bumped in a saddle as a horse springs
        from one diagonal to another,
                a two-beat gait light and balanced
as the four-beats per stride become the hair-blowing,
        wind-in-the-face, grass-rippling,
                muscle-loosening, forward-leaning
        exhilaration of the gallop.

And I have never counted the slow four-beat pace
                of distinct, successive hoofbeats
        in such an order as to be called *The Walk.*
Or learned *capriole, piaffe, croupade* in a riding school,
                nor heard the lingo of outback cattle cutters
        spat out with their whip ends and phlegm.

I have never stepped my hands over the flanks
                of a spotted mare, nor ridden a Cleveland Bay
carriage horse, or a Yorkshire coach horse,
                a French Percheron with its musical snicker,
        or a little Connemara, its face buried
                in broomcorn, or in a bin of Wexford apples.

I have never called a horse Dancer, Seabiscuit, Ned,
Nellie, Trigger or Chester, or made clicking noises
with my tongue during the fifty kilometres
to town with a baulking gelding and a green
quarter-top buggy. Nor stood in a field while
an old nag worked every acre
only stopping to release difficult knobs of manure

and swat flies with her tail. And though I have
waited for jockeys at the backs of stables
in the mist and rain, for the soft feel of their riding silks
and saddles, for the cool smoke of their growth-stunting
cigarettes, for the names of the yearlings
and mares they whisper along with the names
of horse-owning millionaires – ah, more, more even
than them – I have always loved the word *appaloosa*.

The Binoculars

When we heard the news that Harvey Markham
had fallen to his death, my father and I were
walking by the inlet. Ducks strung out in echelon
had come in to dabble and dredge, we were
watching them along with the rise and swirl,
lift and spill, spin and glint of the spindrift
blowing along the shore. Harvey was my father's
oldest friend. For years they'd shared a love
of sea-birds, they'd go almost anywhere for a sighting.
Harvey would always risk the difficult places:
the top of a rocky outcrop, a ledge or bluff
where he could watch the swooping and soaring
of courting pairs of osprey, or see the brood
inside an eagle's nest. Nearly every bird named
in my father's notebooks Harvey had spotted first.
A streaked shearwater, a great and least frigatebird,
a white-faced storm petrel they'd seen almost
as a single sighting one day off a headland
as Harvey zeroed in upon a distant fleck,
then into the crevices in the rocks. Whenever
I thought of Harvey, I'd see his face locked
to his binoculars as he swept the sky to track
some speck to its point of vanishing. His fingers
skilful as an optometrist's, adjusting the scope,
bringing the cliffs in close, or lengthening

his vision outwards, his hands always keeping
his line of sight steady. After Harvey's death
my father locked those binoculars away
in an airless display case along with a frigatebird
he'd paid to have stuffed in the soaring position,
its red throat-pouch in full ballooned display.
Years later, I opened the cabinet. The bird had
slipped its mount and I wanted to set it right,
but first I took out Harvey's field glasses. I levelled
them to the back of the room and saw what looked
to be the sky in mauve-grey, sea mist patterns
full of flecks like the birds I could never bring
to view. I tilted the glasses closer to the light
and saw the dusty, spotted, buff-coloured shells
of falcon eggs and what seemed to be the mottling
on the breast of a grey goshawk. Then I remembered
what decades ago my father had done. Grief
had broken him and for quite some time
he seemed locked away, fixed to a lost field
trying to scan for all the old vignettes intruding
at the edges. I saw him again clasping Harvey's
binoculars between his knees, working the prisms
and the light-gathering lenses he'd removed back
into place – and slowly sealing into each intricate
chamber as much as he could of Harvey's ashes.

Herons at Dusk

This is the time of day when the light runs down the sky
like bluing and meets the bay, when whipbirds set acoustic
flares along the trees, when I'll stand and listen to the yachts,
a sound as if cutlery were being replenished on table tops;

but most of all when I love to watch the herons step along
the shore, how like tai chi performers they will step deftly,
easily into constantly reconfigured stances. I can see one
down by the mangroves now, moving and then redoing

each step as though it has become fastidious about how
to present the curve of is neck, a punctilio it must get right
before it will allow itself to stand twinned to its reflection.
Near the pier another heron is holding its bill over the reeds

as purposeful as a seiner with a marlinespike, before it
jabs then returns to its wire-drawn stance, as if all it must
achieve now is to lift and pull itself into the distance
like sail twine. When the herons quietly step they make

even the stilts' and avocets' neat stabs along the sand
seem like slapstick; they make the routines of all who fish
along the shore at dusk seem over-weighted and vaudevillian.
And look! how they stand – at last – stilled to perfection.

The Mosquito, Riffs and Plaints

I prefer the cicada's stroboscopic glitzy aural brandishing
and the bee's legato burr, even the blowfly's whirr when heat
keeps the pedal down; the cockatoos' pulley-driven clangs

of wrecking-ball metal against a sky – amplified; the wind
as it knocks and turns, knocks and turns and turns into ruin
the slow percussive refrain of the moody, midday rain.

I prefer the digestive grumblings of an eructing city drain,
a frog's slow glugs, bats' incessant chitter, the crickets
like house-slaves singing; even pigeons under the eaves

doing an all-day funked-out coo. I prefer the damaged
ringing of my inner ear, and (yes, say it!) everything
turning tintinnabular than to hear this stylus-burdened

insect-pest mimicking a tiny current's hum and hiss; this
long-nosed diva floating above my breath. Plump criminal,
you idle above the cool pleasure of my skin, you hitch

up your mouthparts, plot crimes above my pulse, steal
from my cask of good deep red. Look, I know what you
courier and it isn't quinine. I know how you lie in gulley

traps, in pit latrines, at the edges of clear running streams.
You love the horse trough, the water butt, puddles in
unmade roads, brick pits, barrow pits, you love the dregs

in rusted tins. Little aching creature stuttering to the night
like a tiny violin, you look like one of Liszt's hemi-demi-semi-
quavers scrawled across night's long stave. With you I count

insomnia's digits, all your mal-arias are buzzing in my blood.
I prefer a storm's drumfire scud, an afternoon's cloud of slow
distempered midges, all the sizzling obituaries of fruit flies

above a compost, the loudest of Frank Zappa's riffs zapping
anything but noise flying through my head. Mosquito, you
sing into my ear as if it were your mosque, but I'm waiting

for you with my aerosols around the back-end of spring.
I'm waiting, Morse-quito, for my hand to slap a message
back – just once, loudly – and quick as your electric dialect.

The Harbour

for Robert Gray

Out on the harbour yachts are clustered like little wedges
of hard white cheese stuck with toothpick-thin masts.
The moon is a cocktail onion, or just a plain soda cracker,
but the sun is a dollop of hot chilli relish floating above

the vol-au-vent shape of Fort Denison. At Cremorne Point
a lighthouse gleams like a salt cellar. Out between the Heads
those white spinnakers are as tautly bellied as garlic cloves.
Now the sun is striking the waffle-grids of office blocks

with a glow thick as pureed apricots. Later down those streets
chocolate-dark shadows will set between the tall servings
of glass, but not before more daylight pours over them
as amply as raspberry syrup over sundaes. Now the wakes

of little boats bring bright florets to the edges of the quay,
sudden as popcorn bursts. The Opera House, standing
out on the point, seems a sumptuous restaurant's arrangement
of prim serviettes, or the divisions of the light-dazzled

wedges of a lemon. I'm watching all this from a balcony
just as the wind gets up, just as I'm remembering your poem,
Robert, about the late ferry crossing the water – and as
the light spills intemperately and wantonly as honey.

The Aquarium

The weirdest things are the tiny cuttlefish,
the ones whose translucent, gelatinous faces
are hung with the rippling curtains
of their feeding tentacles. Their locomotion-frills are wafting too,
fine as chiffon.
The sign says there's a stonefish in this tank,
though you can barely see it
covered with the rocky ornamentations, with the green and lilac
encrustations of the pool itself.
Now a jellyfish pulses by. I can see four white gonads
through the body-wall.
This one's trailing-filaments end in large purple knobs.
I imagine holding a jellyfish
would take a cosmetic surgeon's steady hands,
someone used to manoeuvring
the wobbly sacs of breast implants.

This tank is as glossy and bright as a brochure
of a temperate rocky shore.
It's full of anemones whose tentacles suddenly flare
around the perimeters of their mouths
with the supple, progressive ease of Mexican waves.
The tentacles radiate out in rows
as though they were circles
of colourful, feeding fish.
These sea urchins are as scarlet and as prickly as rambutans,

there are so many, I feel as though I'm peering into the hollow
in a wave-swept reef.

A spotted pipefish drifts out of a hole
and for a moment
looks like a stray strand of kelp or eelgrass you sometimes see
wound through the links of old boat chains.
The tank is also full of skates, stingrays,
eagle rays, stingarees. I watch their edges undulate
with all the yielding tonicity of mollified rubber
as they sweep around the glass.
This skate looks as thick and broad as a tropical leaf;
this one's edges swirl and fan out as if the tank-water
were being pumped with the submerged, weighted rhythms
of cello, oboe
and the slow thrumming of a lyre.

On its underside, this stingray has two dark spiracles
and deep gill-slits set in its bright white skin.
It could almost be a ghost floating around a cold, wide ceiling
with that quadrangular disc-shape
changing, fading away almost to nothing at the edges.

Two turtles are swimming together
and suddenly I remember:
The dance was slow, was slow, was slow. Slow was the dance, very.
The dancer turned, her arms held out as she came closer, slowly.

An eel projects its long-tubed nostrils out of a crevice.
Its head is thin, compressed, swollen
                    behind the eyes.
I step back when it unrolls across the glass like a stocking full
      of slime.

Now blue-finned leatherjackets, big-eye trevally, candy wrasse,
painted anglerfish, grouper and rock whiting
            do another circuit of the tank.
      Their pictures are displayed around the perimeter
like mugshots of fleshy-lipped, thick-browed thugs.
A small fortune of aqua light is falling into the tank, making it glow
like a milky sapphire, like mother-of-pearl.

In the next tank I watch an octopus luxuriate in its own arms,
then languidly roll them around itself as if it were looking
            for a loophole,
            then it loosely lets them out
far beyond its head and mantle, each arm moving as though it had
      taken up a quill
and were writing over and over in slanting, looping letters:
            lollygag, lollipop, lollapalooza
on the tank-water, on the pebbles and the rising stream of bubbles.

Down the ramp there is a pool of seals
and one has worked its way onto the platform where later it will
      perform

by keeping a ball balanced on its nose
while clapping its flippers;
from here it looks as shiny as a piece of sculpted tourmaline.

I walk to the next tank and watch a platoon of cruising
gummy sharks. A mass of aerating bubbles
is pouring like a small Milky Way over their backs as they slide
up to the surface – they do not know about the length
of purchase the bubbles, sand or glass
will have on their days. A grey nurse shark glides forward
with an air of absolutism.
Its mouth seems a fortification, a compound. It commands
its regiment of fins, but looks so unreal, lifeless,
as though it were made of fibreglass, or some seamless
polished plastic.

I go back to watch the octopus again whose arms now
seem to be conducting music to four distinct orchestras.
Then it plays with one of the small rings put there for its
amusement
and in a flash
as though it were a length of voile or Dacca silk, it draws
all four metres of itself through the ring's small hole
shape-shifting then tightening
its small face against the glass before it holds the rim
of the ring again, and it draws itself back through
as if into another portal, another hole in space.

But even after this, it's that shark I can't forget –
how its eyes keep staring, colder than time – how it never stops swimming,
how it never closes its mouth.

New Poems

Revisiting the Bay

i.m. Dorothy Porter

I rarely come here now, once or twice since you died.
Today a storm is brewing, lightning flashes repeatedly –
a tabloid camera at high vantage snatching salacious shots.
I walk to the headland, to the lighthouse where gulls
are blowing centrifugally off its top. Here we'd stand
watching birds, watching yachts luff when the wind

thwacked their pale sailcloth; the small ferry curmurring
by the dock always as reliable as the midday heat,
or the three o'clock nor'easterly gust. We'd pick up pebbles,
hurl them from the bluff, our ballast against ill-luck.
Now, the clinking of spoons and plates carries up
from the shorefront cafés – it's as if they're tattling

on the gaiety of one of our afternoon-long conversations.
Wind cuts across the bay, yacht masts scribble: script
doctors changing cast and plot, but not the bustling
backdrop of the sea with its quarrelling waves,
nor my vision of you on top of the windy, tussocky cliff
hurling pebbles, happy, laughing, saying blessings for us.

Walking in the Reserve

The casuarinas and apple gums are full of honeyeaters,
chaffering finches, crows sounding their adenoidal *kaar-aar,*
kaar-aar, and currawongs with bubbling sub-songs and mellow
silver flutings. It's summer, the cicadas pulsate as loudly
as the council's irrigation sprinklers turning with jet propulsion

over the grass. We all ache for an off-button – but turn
the bend and everything quietens: a heron looks as if it's within
contemplative striking-distance of an ineffable mystery.
Wood ducks daddle, settle where a runnel thins and trickles,
scat-sings over pebbles. An egret takes off, creaking like an oar

just as a boat's wash shepherds swamp hens upstream,
and wind in the reeds whispers *jeezus, sweet jeezus,*
I'm short of breath and sleepless. At the next turn, round,
silver webs – as if someone had lasered a stack of CDs
into the finest openwork, then tossed them into the branches.

Butcherbirds call *rusty stuff, rusty stuff* as if trying to high-tune
a stretch of old fence wire; then they flip sagas and twang
open a riff of bluegrass. But it's the magpies I love, calling
as if lowering a bucket into a creek, pulling it up, cool and welling,
then tippling there. A sound on tap in the morning and at dusk.

Dusk

A praying mantis is stalking a caterpillar
micro-nicking its way along the jasmine.
Close up, the caterpillar is as black
and furry as mould on ten-day-old bread –
move back, it's a teased-out skein of wool
wicking the evening dew.
Suddenly the mantis pulls up its knees,
rests its serrated feet against its abdomen
and intensely rocks – it looks
as if it's about to shimmy, or break-dance
on spring-loaded legs. Then it stops,
waits, steadies its head, calms its quivering
body – a compass needle aligning north.
Next it holds out its arms as if it were
about to take up a baton… The caterpillar
is shuffling, a slow boogaloo, pulling
no burden, except its unperceived death.

To My Neighbour's Hens

Clara and Claudia, I hope you always stare
at nothing in particular, taking turns through the garden
savouring angelica, borage and thyme. I hope you
always gussy up your tail feathers towards a proud
Rock Cornish rooster who has a rubicund comb,
a deep-burnished chest and an oratorical voice.
May you always scratch at the earth among
the ordinary sounds of tree branches swaying,
dogs barking, leaves blowing, and never have
to live on a sloping wire floor with six other birds
in a space the size of a filing cabinet drawer,
your beaks cut off, all of you starved, bald,
mad, never seeing daylight. May your male chicks
never be snatched away from you and put through
a high-speed grinder, mixed with hormones
and fed to you, making you grow faster than your bodies
can cope with before you are trucked off to slaughter,
the sky cracking inwards like an egg. May you
always walk through yard-light and the rain's grainy
footage and sleep on butter-coloured straw
where you watch tufts of your down drift
through sunshafts, knowing nothing about battery
cages, the jets of water that scald away
feathers, or the motorised blades that slit throats.
May you always be fed corn, oatmeal, spaghetti,

chow mein and risotto leftovers, the crusts
of toast and dark pumpernickel, green and yellow
kitchen scraps into which genial, attentive humans
have mixed the shells of your own good eggs.

Flying Foxes, Wingham Brush

for Deborah Bird Rose

Some of the bats are elbowing their way
along the branches, a collection of broken
business umbrellas. Some hang like charred

pods, or look like furry oriental fruit
wrapped in silk sashes. Others are handling
the stretch of their black elastomer wings

as carefully as women checking for snags
in their stockings, ready to step out for the night.
But the smell of the place – decades

of urine, faeces, birth fluids, rotting body
parts and figs, putrid as a munitions factory
with its cloying nitrates, its biting ammonia.

At dusk when the bats take off, the sky
becomes a long sheet of gothic lettering –
some won't return, they'll swing by their

feet on high wires, doomed stuntmen
still in their leathers. Newly orphaned bats,
grief-stricken, will roost on Hills hoists,

snuggle against the lingerie and socks,
the sharp metal squeaks sounding like calls
from their mothers. Some believe bats

are demons' hand puppets, the souls of
unburied infants, death-messengers nibbling
at the edges of our dreams, but I love to listen

to them sending out their clicks and squeaks,
flying under the moon, the crystal brew
of stars; how after sweeping upwards, they'll

backtrack to parks, yards, hearing all the angles
and contours in our gardens, soliloquising
their way through tunnels and labyrinths,

weighing their love of nectar with the love
of night-flight – scent-resonators
of the season. Now high in these branches

they're as chatty as children fuelled by
afternoon sugars. They hug themselves lightly,
closely, the way tree-lovers hug wood.

Native Orchids

We'd come as far as the wooden bridge, not too far
from town – rows of windows in the distance like strip cartoons,
and the moon in one frame, a dab of correction fluid.

We'd come to find native orchids, though I'd begun
to believe they existed in places none of us would see,
not unless we entered magic circles and danced

ceremoniously with wine cups in our hands, hallucinating
ourselves as gods. Someone said they'd seen native orchids
in a book, that they looked like psychedelic spiders.

We walked past the creek, trudged over rocks and grass,
soft grey moths fluttering at our heels; then to an overhang;
below in the creek, tadpoles like free-floating

commas, and an egret still as a porcelain ewer full
of cool wine, a chestnut teal shaking water from its head
as though trying to free itself from some witless tenet.

When cockatoos massed onto branches strutting, screeching,
fanning out their crests with the bluster of card-sharps
playing bluff hands, we were glad to walk on, despite

a standing army of leeches, a cloud of gnats moving
like a constantly revolving door. Cicadas had begun a high-
torsional jamming session in the apple gums: still

no orchids, though we did see a flower with filaments
fine as caterpillar lint, a tiny insect gear-shifting
its legs as it roamed the seed-freighted pistil and poked

its feelers outside the pinhole edge. A man in the group,
his stomach like a huge puffball bulging over his belt,
kept kicking the caps off toadstools and tearing down

spiders' webs. When at lunch he sat near a bull ants'
nest, none of us said a thing, we just watched him
jump, trying to escape his own nerve-ends that were

taking him on a brutal expedition of incendiary pain.
The group leader, a woman with oceanic blue hair,
her cheeks speckled like a martin's egg, lowered her

head to the ground and with her boot flipped over
a rock. Again no orchids, just a centipede, a scurrying
cutting of brown fern. When we returned to the road,

we saw the late sun syndicating its light in level after
level of office block windows – and for a moment
we were startled out of ourselves, the way we might

have been had we seen the orchids' red, shell-pink
or turquoise petals… The eastern sky was now plum-purple,
fruit bats filling it like cinders from a woodland blaze.

The Boathouse

ending on a line by John Burnside

No one on the boats, just cats – thin, furtive.
There's the blown cry of terns and the wheedling
embarkations of crows, but you will not slip

the knot of your thoughts, what has brought you
to this harbour. Rain in the distance, the same
cold chant echoing in your steps, in the oars

and in the salt-incrusted timbers of the boats
pitching by the pier. The smell of diesel, rust,
bilge. A pelican hunkers down in the wind

near a tangle of broken nets, lines, seaweed,
an oily squalor of wash along the shore.
From the boathouse fishermen with voices

like spray looming through a blowhole,
their weather-knotted faces turning to leer at you.
One of them, stiff as old rope, dumps

a bucket of guts and fish heads on the boards.
The cats come quickly, eyeing each other, hissing,
clearing the pylons of gulls. Below the pier,

a stingray's slow, soothing undulations.
Now the cats slink away with the waste
and like a mass of flies your thoughts return –

blatant, insistent – back to when you'd walk
into cold spindrift, or on to the rocks from where
the whole rank harbour was visible, the boathouse

with its splintering boards, ruined paint, always
a man on the jetty peering into the water…
In the distance a sudden lance of sunlight reveals

the ambiguity of your coming and going;
how the stone's throw of the past is still at your feet
and will not move, though now you walk away

from the pier. A sharp skreel – yacht-repair,
or the noise of returning gulls. Sand grains
blow as savagely as fish hooks against your legs.

A cat trails you, its pitiful cry mingling with
the stink of dreck and rotting weed… both of you
homing in on something – the urgency of elsewhere.

Hymnal / Wild Bees

i.m. Martin Harrison

As the water scats over pebbles, as the creek thins
and trickles, there's a sound that seems pirated
from a flock of seed-gathering parrots and a muster
of hot-gospelling crows. Along the mud spoonbills

scribble, their bills as frenetic as compass needles
trying to orienteer quick passage. It's the egrets
I watch most – poised, quiet as Gilbertine nuns,
who with naked feet, seem about to step along

a corridor and enter their prayer cells. I don't come
here often – there are spiders, ticks, thick-bellied
snakes, and toadstools as bloodless as the fingers
of morticians' gloves. Once I saw a headless possum,

then a pit bull mauling a lizard it had clawed out
from the dampness of a log. There are trails
of bull ants talking chemically and incessantly
to each other, bits of repeating code, and where

the melaleucas leak tannin into the runnels, you'd
swear it was a spill of beef's blood. But sometimes
I like to come and notice how the spore-cases
of the bracken are like hemmings of brown wool,

or to smell the leaf rot curated along the path
by hard-working organisms. Mostly I come
to watch bees fly around the high heat of their hive
and swarm their weight towards the gum blossoms

in a light soot of yellow. Today I see that the limb
housing the hive has fallen, shattered. Some bees
lie trapped in the sticky spill. Some bees will have
fled with the queen. This hive, once a murmuring

blood-warm gourd, is silent and I'll never see again
the bees among the wildflowers, or see them busy
in the depths among the stamens, moving from cup
to cup as though they were flames lighting candles.

I'll never hear their lingering vibrato, a mind enamoured
of its own music, getting right each thought's hum,
its bearing and its course. Bees no longer alive or high
in their hive, no longer making clear elaborated nectar.

Banaras Silk

They say you can never forget its weightless drape
over your arm, your shoulder; that it will make you ache
for ruby-pink wine and night-long rapture; that if you
touch it to your lips you will only ever speak truth.

They say its rustling is the most seductive sound –
a whispering of the Ganges when it ebbs and flows
among rushes. They say it's colourless until you wear it,
and then, if your heart is pure, one by one the threads

become rainbows. Some say the colours only come
into fullness when a sitar is played, or a silver flute,
or when you forget your restless thoughts, when you
ask yourself the great questions naked, when you talk

to sparrows and to the shadows on your bedroom wall,
when you air your fears at the same time as you feed
your joys. They say its perfume will make you swoon,
but only if you don't desire it, and only if you wear

the silk during a difficult inward journey from which
you'll return either as a poet or a hermit, renouncing
wine and clothes, as you look up into a thankless
sky, and then cloak yourself in self-control and grief.

Grasses

for Stephen

Earth's the right place for love
ROBERT FROST

If given the chance, my sweet, to wander
through a wavering field with you, what grasses
would I choose? Perhaps gentle Annie, eulalia,
plumerillo, walloo, or mountain wanderrie.

We could spend an afternoon in the beach grass,
or the one-year-grass and speak of seasons;
or stroll down a hill of jabbers and spangle top
where magpies and currawongs sing like a brook.

Or we could lie on quealed leaves and dream
of walking in Yass tussock at dusk, chewing
on long stems as we watch the sun appear
from behind slow-shifting clouds, a light wind

purring in Tabookie grass like run-off after rain.
Beautiful to watch the autumn moon shine
on the plume-headed pampas, or see the sun's
chiffon haze upon jointed-bottle-washers,

knotty-butt neverfail and gardener's garters.
Listen, the lovegrass is shivering – I can hear
the touch of our trespass. Yes, earth is the best
place for love, earth and the vivacious grasses.

Lighthouse Beach

The first drops of rain mottle the concrete –
slowly beach umbrellas collapse like the tents
of an old empire. The sun too has shrivelled from its allegiance
to summer and slipped behind a cloud swinging in
on crinkling cables. Out by the rocks rain

hits the cliffs – a sound as if rescue helicopters
with steel winches were trying to haul up the heaving sea's
white crests. The windows of the houses mounting
the hill repeat the same reflection: a smokeless
running sky stoked by the devil's pitchforks.

Thunder's carnal rumbling is filling the streets
while the rain marches with the swagger of recruits
fast gaining rank… On the headland a lighthouse
stands still as an altarpiece, then for a moment,
sea-misted, it looks like a whale's spout

about to give way to wind and waves; but then –
staunch, impregnable: defending itself against rain's
incessant recitation of possession and rhythm,
against wind's high wheedling, against midsummer's
affiliations with another scurrilous black squall.

By the Shore

after the painting 'Blue Yellow and White'
by Jack Carington Smith

The yachts are so elegant. If only you could let the day
take you away – you hanker to scud out of earshot
of your future, fall into the full fetch of the bay. Instead
you're anchored to a tiny tot. You have tired legs,

an aching back. Your seat of sand has turned cold
while you've watched your daughters. Look, you could
be a girl yourself. That small row boat calls you to step
into it and sleep, be coddled by sunlight and wind –

the whole day yours to dream about yachts, little skiffs
of vim and mischief swirling on a harbour of shot silk
and bonnet-blue waves. In a moment your newborn
will cry to be nursed. You'll curse the water, its quiet

surge, those yachts in the distance, full of stately
calm. If only you could lie down in the bobbing boat
you'd see the sky, finally yours… So close, that hull
angled to the ocean, so bright in the quarterlight.

Waterlily Pond

for Diana Bridge

At the slow-gaited end of summer's day,
dragonflies dart as precisely as needles
tatting the ornate patterns of lace-charts.
A kingfisher snatches a dragonfly midair –
holds it in its bill like an ampoule
of iridescent magenta ink. Slowly
an egret lifts – smoke from a clutch
of joss sticks. Koi sip at the surface, their lips
like the rubber rings of party balloons.
Another egret rises, legs trailing
under it long and thin as toasting forks.
A damselfly in rapid flight, a scholiast's pen
annotating in margins, stops, touches
down on a lotus just as a heron
steps with the calm posture of a Shinto priest
about to cleanse a shrine with prayer.
An ibis swallows what it's caught
from leaf pulp and bottom slime. I hear
the polyphonic tinkling of water, a tiswas
of insects soft-pedalling above white stones.

Driving to Broken Hill

Distance – continuous, ungestured. Crows
on fence-wire-watch stretching into a haze.
When a kestrel hovers it's an abundance –
like water, or a horizon with a hill.
We pass towns, streets written-off by dogs
and half-asleep dreamers. Those who live
at the edges here must have put aside
all satisfaction; mile after mile of paddocks
full of saltbush and wrong conclusions.
The heat keeps drawing wobbling lines
parallel to forgetting. We think of rooms
by the sea as we drive, no props in this theatre
of emptiness, only a whistling kite
or two, trucks hurtling on interstate haul.
At dusk, more kangaroos, unblinking,
holding their pose, stunned into road kill –
the highway's only intimacy. We hear insects
smack against our windows with thwarted
wanderlust. The horizon glowing red
is not what we can attach desire to, though
perhaps a sky strung with starlight, a vault
of curative silver, will be enough to ease
the choking flatness, the ubiquitous dust.

Sugarcane Juice

The same song in the hands/ as in the mouth

NIALL CAMPBELL

She juices limes and lemons then turns
the mangle to crush the sugarcane. Her bangles
tinkle as she pounds cardamom and ginger,

then adds some mint and cloves. I can smell
the pinch of cinnamon she quickly mixes in
before she sieves the contents through a scrim.

Now with tongs she clinks some ice cubes
into a pitcher, rubs pink salt along its rim.
I watch the dance of her hands as she wipes

her tray of glasses clean; those thin, high
squeaks, like her voice, spruiking the juice,
calling us in. She's careful to pour every

glass full, she who makes us feel like nectar
birds arriving at her fragrant stand. The same
song in our mouths that was in her hands.

Rory

We'd often see Rory outside the shed trying
to classify clouds coming in on the evening wind –
clouds he thought were the farm's clip
of fine-grained wool. On clear blue days
he'd strike match after match and try to class
the smoke. My aunt would say, 'There's Rory
again, tricking ghosts.' She'd told me years ago
anthrax had turned his arms and legs black
as land scorched with fire – *woolsorter's disease*
they called it then.
                These days he'll look up,
sigh, walk as if he's carrying a bale's weight
of wool towards a skirting table, his fingers
feeling the air as if he were assessing the wool fat,
the tightness of the crimp, inspecting it
for burr and frib. The shearers tease him,
say his mind's turned soft as felt. Some days
when the sky is full of wispy cirrus, Rory
will say that some new shedhand has forgotten
to sweep away the britch wool from the shearing.
Sometimes you can hear him auctioning
off his bales, his prices unyielding,
his tone as twangy as a ring of blowflies.
Winter mornings he's out with his arms raised
into a dense batting of fog. On summer days
he'll be reaching towards a haze, even bushfire smoke,

or looking into the distance for stray clouds,
ready to coax them in like orphaned lambs.
Once one of the shearers stuck a mess of dags
and cotted wool to Rory's head, then took to him
with rusty shears to do some wigging.
My uncle punched the man so hard he reeled
round the yard like a wether with the ryegrass staggers.
Sometimes – when we catch Rory looking up
at a line of cumulus coming in – we smile
and say, 'There's Rory *wool-gathering* again.'

The Pest Inspector

Small, compact, Grigore crawled easily
into tight spaces. In his white overalls
he looked soft and milky – a giant termite.
He was friendly, talked about his work:
'houses so full of cockroaches
it sounded as though you were walking
on potato chips.' He gave good advice:
'Listen at night and if you hear a sound
as though you've left a record on
after all the songs have played, the clicking
of a needle as it tracks in a groove;
if you hear what you take to be
the scratchings of a mouse, the contractions
of a cooling tin roof, click beetles
snapping their body parts to flip themselves
right way up – take note, they could
turn out to be the mandible-crafted ticks
of termites eating along the grain of your floorboards.'
He showed us how to rap on door-frames
and walls: 'If the response is papery or hollow
– don't play AC/DC, Queen, Led Zeppelin,
Kiss, Deep Purple, or Black Sabbath –
hard rock makes termites eat wood
twice as fast.' We'd laugh – he knew
our tastes were light classical and southern soul.
His were show tunes and Bulgarian folk.

I'd listen to him humming as he tapped
his way along the joists and rafters, or threw
a handful of rat baits into the roof cavity.
Once he took out a photo of a termite queen
'from an upmarket bar in Bangkok – long
as my thumb, dipped in rice wine, served live.'
Last month when someone else turned up,
I asked about Grigore – the man told
me he'd died on the job after finding
a concealed nest of European wasps.
I thought of the pain pounding through
him like a bass riff of death metal,
his heart going into asymmetric rhythm
like a morose folk dance from the Thracian plain.
I mourned him that evening playing
Chopin and Sam & Dave to the walls
and floorboards, witnesses to his light touch,
his voice humming *If I Were a Rich Man,*
his favourite refrains from *Annie Get Your Gun.*

Sun Music

I

I remember on a coastal walk how I watched
my father, for the first time, tip a gift pair
of binoculars to his face; how his eyes drank
in the sky, those light-filled cylinders giving
him the weightless soaring of kites and eagles.
After that he was a changed man.
He filled each weekend with this long-distance
intimacy, coring into the soft stratum
of sea-mists for sea-birds. I mostly stayed
around the coves, watching dogs chase pelicans,
or ibis come in to land, their leathery heads
looking like bones from a peat bog burial.
My father had begun searching for himself
along the cliffs, the part of himself he'd lost
to the bottled depths of his drinking.
We were glad to see binoculars rather than
beer cans, or hip flasks as the first thing
he packed for an outing. Now, he was intoxicated
by the sea, the sky, the spindrift a new
spell he could steer his life by, at dawn or dusk,
at low tide when stilts and tattlers roamed
along a sand bar, or an egret posed like a too-slim
model in the glossy light. The birds
he recorded in his notebooks marked the days
he'd begun to lift his gaze from the blurred

bottom of a whisky glass, a lens always
trained on grief and failure. Osprey, Brahminy kite,
swamp harrier, Pacific baza, brown falcon,
frigate bird, godwit, figbird, rufous night heron:
new sightlines, prospects, better fields of view.
I can still see him on our summer holidays
lifting sky-filled lenses to his face,
mouth agape, searching peppertrees and wattles
for pied butcherbirds unfurling the joy
of morning in their throats, high arias holding
the river's light, the audible workings of the sun.

2

So many birds around this bay: godwits, stilts
oyster catchers, tattlers, avocets, a gannet
flying by the side of a ketch, pelicans circling
before their feet lisp into the water near the isthmus.
I lengthen my lens deeper into the distance –
osprey, a red-tailed tropic bird. I sit by the dock
as the horn of a ferry explodes a flock of seagulls,
a few cockatoos on the roof of the yacht club
screeching out a burst of crested complaint.
The bay trembles through its mood-swings of colour:
cerulean, azure, oyster, lead, pewter. An eagle,
perhaps a Brahminy kite, drifts like a floater
in my line of sight. There are trinket sounds
of yachts whose sails, later, will race like quills
taking shorthand, or scribbling odd hieroglyphs.

Here the shore is clinkered with soldier crabs,
and egrets, cautious, mannered, stepping
as if the day has been bestowed upon them
as a regal right. Yesterday they stood in the thin
corsetry of the rain, the water flat and colourless
as paraffin-coated paper. By the boatshed, a dog
wobbles its nostrils to separate the stink of dead fish
from the reek of diesel, the smell of rope from rusted wire –
a fish scale stuck to its nose like a tiny salted porthole.
A pelican skims along the tide – a susurration
like an afternoon breeze blowing through a casuarina –
then it steps with clownish swagger along the pier.
A few fishermen chat, then emptied of words,
dial into the silence with their reels. There'll be a storm
soon – lightning falling like lopped tree limbs,
the wind in hyper drive conducting a confused choir
of masts; lights like cash-points coming on at the hotels
on the other side of the bay. Suddenly a heron
steps out from under one of the pylons
holding a soldier crab in its bill as though it were
a bright blue badge from the Guild of Diligent
Shore Walkers, patient attendants of shallows and tides.
The dog from the boathouse follows me,
its tail striking insects from the grass, its bark
as it chases seagulls, a pastiche of the low vowels
of a brush bronzewing and a rock pigeon.
Its owner calls out – his voice is like rain on a tin awning,
a clash of gutturals and sibilants as the dog's name

is shouted before it turns and runs with loping ardour
back to the boatshed to sit and curl upon itself, a coil
of old rope. More egrets gather – grandees and slim
duchesses walking on legs like tightened lute strings,
the imprints of their feet ratifying their possession
of the shore. A flock of pigeons occupy the grass,
in the sunlight their neck feathers have that mineralised
sheen of oil patches on a wet road. I love to walk
these deckled shores, binoculars lightly perched
on my face as I watch godwits work a line
of retreating water, osprey circle around the cliffs,
hawks find amplitude on thermals, these lenses
helping me scope new images and thoughts, ones
that breed and flit joyously through my head,
each speck dilating into fullness. No more
am I squinting into the monocular bottom of a bottle,
or into the myopic base of a liquor-filled tumbler,
but filling my sights with beauty and distance.
Now I listen as a pied butcherbird, like a jazz flautist
in the trees, works on syncopated chimes and ensemble
phrases, its liquid crystal voice – music from the sun.

Ode to Ambergris

Fresh ambergris, old ambergris, any sort will do:
ambergris with the dark earthy scent of pine bark
and mulch, ambergris smelling like oak moss
and smoke. The best grade of grey, the poorest
of black; chalky or spongy, waxy or hard; ambergris
weathered by air, sun and salt. Fresh ambergris,

old ambergris, any sort will do. Even the black
will tease out an odour, hoodwink the nose to hold
a note longer, fix the caprice of all fickle scents.
If you grind ambergris – fresh ambergris, old ambergris –
down to the core, then mix it with sugar, civet
and musk and place it in horse dung for twenty-nine

days, you get a strong essence, slow to evanesce.
Perfumers will pay top money for any sort, any
sort at all – fresh ambergris, old ambergris – ambergris
mottled like marble, ambergris that smells faintly
marine then smells like ploughed earth, ambergris
that looks like old cheese and smells even worse.

Clouds

I'm tired of these endless highfalutin blue skies –
I want clouds common as whisked egg-whites
or mashed marshmallows on a plate. Clouds that by dusk

are the colour of fish-gutters' gloves. I want dissenting
thunderheads with their cloud-to-cloud lightning,
clouds recruited from monsoonal lows and Scotch mist,

clouds circumnavigating the planet then signing up
for Greenpeace. I want clouds to resist the oligarchic reign
of blue and come striding in like men and women

who fling their bodies against dirt, then get up praising
the wings of birds. Clouds whose fluffy tops kiss in public.
Clouds cantering off to horse latitudes, magnanimous

in manner, riding low. I want blue skies to admit their
bumbling stewardship and own up to their enormous cost.
One by one I call the clouds in. A cloud for each child

hungry, naked. A cloud for those in war-ravaged places
where shadows terrorise doorways and the old live
between rubble and crumbled bread. Blue skies will

break the windows of your house; they will offer you
their emptiness and your life at a knock-down price, their lips
will pronounce only names written in expensive ink.

Let the clouds come and cross over each other, scrubbing
away the ubiquitous azure that remembers nothing
except the value of the moon's silverware and the silken

dreams of dictators and their priests. In the distance
two clouds are touching, twisting into a lintel of sanctuary
where the blue can't trespass. I want clouds thick

as laundry, handkerchief-clouds waving fondly
as we drive away towards fields, waterfalls and laughter,
sick of counting the cerulean jewels on the ocean.

A good cloud will precipitate the deepest source
of our moral passion, our principal wisdom.
Blue skies rebuke all who come down from the burning

mountains, those who believe in snowflakes,
rainforests, turtles, the scorpion's sting, who know
the heat calving the glaciers is as convincing as pain.

Peterhead

East coast, Scotland

Far-out – whitecaps, wind, a few boats, gulls
as querulous as orienteers in bleak weather.
The moon a fillet of whiting lying in a sky
of sour ice. Stone houses, side streets

with shadows limping like cruelled dogs.
In corners, light is stacked – obsolete weaponry.
But I've come here to be with the shadows,
the wind and the cold, dark harbour

and the clouds more shabby and broken
than the council flats. There's history
in the fissured cliffs, in the light the air rusts
at dusk. I can see my father in the armoury

of his youth, striding along these streets.
But *the town that sinks, sinks us all,* someone
said. And the future settled in with its awful
weather, its injuries, and its sea-breath.

Resort Town

Sunset here is the distant roar of motorbikes,
and down Pacific Street I hear the enormous rage
that fills the mosquito's head.
Flies still circle in the day's unalterable groove.
A gull pierces the distance like a sail needle.

Summer's already gone
with its squalls and king tides, quarrels between breakers
and shore. In the palm fronds, a windy shoot-out –
cockatoos firing gunmetal
screeches into the dusk. At the marina boats called *Insolence,*

Betrothal, Party Girl, Gypsea, Liquidity bob in the swell,
their masts angle like competing
violin bows – those principal instruments which must be heard
above all others. On the headland motels light up
like bright perfume bottles

selling sex – headlights flare like shoals of jellyfish
then cruise away. On the beach's far end – pylons in tight
barnacle socks, pelicans lumbering
where a few old men hold fishing rods and all evening
listen to the irascible abrading of their reels

along with the crickets.
Youths throw bottles into the surf – they know the fast language
of money is spoken only in the casinos and restaurants
and by those who own the shopping malls
and boats. They listen to the tide struggling over the sand bar,

their eyes coined in the beer bottle glass breaking
along the rocks with the force
of their curses. Now a few gulls, like last season's junked fliers,
peel away in the wind; the moon writes its graffiti
in silver glyphs across the hoarding of the cliff.

Fogbow, Scotland

for my father

Nothing looks more full of sorrow
than this pale arc of light on the mist beyond the sea wall –
a rainbow drained of colour. And I know

if the wind scoured deeper there'd be a pentimento
inside the frame: islands on the horizon,
kittiwakes daubed in chalk, the past a sketch

of louring rain. We walk the length
of the esplanade, smell the herring and cod stacked
on the pier, hear water splash, a sullen laughter:

still no view – only a cold offering of white –
a wholesale transmigration of colour to the afterlife.

A Garden in Amsterdam

Amsterdam could not have been more perfect,
over wintering your temperament and your bulbs.
We lived in the one cocoon spun by two silkworms.
Look, your face has become the icon
        of this ruined garden –
I've seen you stare into the shadowlands,
but shut your eye to a stone, a flower, a star.
Yesterday when we walked along the canals,
I pointed out the twigs of the honey locusts
        rubbing together,
a small bewitching music, you flung your scarf
another turn around your neck and spoke
of the motor of war, of your friend the Ambassador's
new expense agenda, then emboxed
in your coat, you walked
to the stall to buy chestnuts poached in syrup.
You were sulking, churlish, you wouldn't share.
You were fastidiously exact practising your accent,
your phrases. You wanted to put an apostrophe
        into every word,
make each word reflexive of your desire to possess.
Even your tendernesses were acts of translation.
Your will was a hammer, external and violent.
I was not ready for how you'd tether me
        with your silking,

nimble need. You were all technique, camouflaged
by a genius for jerrybuilding truth with lies.
I was contaminated, ruined, addicted to counting
ornaments visible through windows. Mist rising
        was ascetic and unbearable.
The swans I saw as white blossoms iced into
solitude and tragedy. Yes, it's too late to live guilelessly,
but at least I don't mock the sparrows
with affected primness, or waste my breath
        on moody requiems
for all my fine spun plans turned threadbare.
You foozling with that lot from the Spanish Club –
I tell you they only liked your expense account
and your skill for saying nothing too woe begotten
        in your fashionable clothes.
The waterwheels, the canals, the lindens,
the copper beeches, the footsteps echoing
in the darkness – all those images by which I found
my way back to you cannot be erased, but now
        I know all your masquerades
and there's always another bridge, another
staircase, another window through which I can watch
someone dust their brittle figurines. There are
still bulbs wintering. There are still sparrows.

A Panegyric for Toads

These slumlords of burrows and tree-hollows
are on the move, dozens of pulsing lung sacs,
'a little ventriloquism of ducks' singing in the spring.

Folklore says the toad's a shape-shifter – rancour
and primeval trouble in its head, devil worship
on its tongue, its third eyelid perpetually wiping

away the sight of ghosts. A toad will leave a glaze
of poison on your hand, but you can forgive it
for this – look at those copper-red eyes leasing

fire to the damp core of evening; listen to their calls
in the reeds like the low-plucked strings of ouds;
and how, sometimes, as if led by an unseen conductor,

sensing peril, their singing instantaneously stops.
At first their mating will look like a congregational
laying on of hands, whose purpose, you could

think, is not to spawn, but to heal their warts.
Some say toads are always belching, breaking
wind, eating each other's shed skin. I'd happily

kiss a toad on her sullen, troglodyte mouth
before she begins her walk to the slime-scented pond
where she must climb over a thick layer

of frogspawn, then scrumming indissolubly
with a group of males, an iron-lock embrace
they won't break for days, risk drowning for sex.

Unlike frogs loaded with the rapid taut and release
of slingshot legs, toads like us, must land-walk,
eat with short tongues, bull their way across earth.

Warmth

i.m. Vera Newsom

1

All day and all night rain falls – it drips down the windows
        as her fingernails tap on a half-empty decanter.
The sound cuts across the room to where her shoes wait, two feet
from the door. She could go out, but she might lose her footing
        on slicked leaves. She picks up a book,

spends a long time with each page. The cat purrs beside her.
She looks into its pupils: thin, black streaks – and hears
        the rain again falling as sharp as cutlery
on the outside bricks. She lets the book slip from her lap,

        runs her fingers over the cat's head and back.
She's glad of the cat, its breathing, its resonant cry primed
to the second string of a violin. She smiles as rain's overtones
        give way to more of its purring, and she brings
a small glass of whisky, warm as conversation, to her lips.

2

It's almost the equinox, grass seed is winnowed
by the wind and the light across the oval is a thick smear
of sunflower butter. The cockatoos come screeching in

like a press gallery turbo-charged by gossip and scandal.
In the distance a flock of turning pigeons makes the sky
flicker like a TV screen. Noon is a dynasty consigned

to jasmine and a delirious militia of bees. The sun
shines in a long sweep over trees and the blue twists
of the harbour. She has walked down the long hill

to hear sea spray bulleting up from the rocks and gulls
jinking around the masts of the boats. Later she may lay
down the lines of a poem with equal agility and rhythm.

As she walks home she thinks of when, under a cover
of wood, she'll be communing with the dirt, part of
her already returned to the air, to the earth, perhaps

in the tiny curled casts of worms, perhaps in the grass
as the stems and caps of mushrooms, or as the rootstock
of bracken and its spores, or even as a puffball smoking

after being pressed between a curious child's finger
and thumb. She is not sad, the day is too lovely,
birds are calling as if someone were throwing coins

into the throats of bells. She sees that the windows
of the office blocks beyond the harbour's petite, cerulean
distance are being flame-grilled by the afternoon sun.

Young Male Lyrebird at the Illawarra Treetop Fly

He has his medley nearly ready. He has pieced together
his own fantasia, even if just from the sound of an owl
regurgitating a pellet of bat fur, a park ranger's
jangling keys, the creak of cable strain when bored,

high-mettled youths jump up and down along the steel
walkway's cantilevered arm. So much he has swept
into his listening, though he's too young to know what
song will quicken the hens, but he doubles his gallantry

if he doubles his song, so soon he'll add a clicking
of insects, rain's braided glissade down the tall trunks
of gums, the barking of a dog, the knocking of possums
on timeworn wood. Perhaps, visitor, one day you might

hear played back with amplification, your own deep
intake of breath that day you saw him raising his tail
into a silver harp, trembling it as he inverted it over
his body, leaping in time to one more mix of an engine

with the twittering of a yellow-faced robin; a whipbird
laying down a lash of whistle-whetted alarm; the multi-
tracking of parrots and wrens with a power saw – there
poised on a stage, accurately taking the day's dictation.

Crows, Calling

Sometimes I hear in the sound of their flying
the breath of a mild emphysemic labouring to climb
a few stairs – and now as I hear one of the flock

drop a call that seems forged from case-hardened
steel nails screeching down a blackboard
I don't surprise myself in thinking also of acoustic

distress flares, or of the strangled aerophonics
of a leaky bagpipe. But no matter which way
I try to make strange whimsy out of their calls

I always hear in them something perverse:
a hacked-out cough going up a smokestack;
a dubbed soundtrack of havoc; a rock band

back-masking satanic lyrics onto vinyl; the hideous
bleating of newborn lambs whose eyes
are being swallowed. Sometimes I hear scenes

from *The Birds*: children under raven attack
from the sky; or I imagine Hitchcock's horror
berating of Tippi Hedren on the set before his voice

is remastered by her tears. Today in the trees
behind my house nothing will mend their tongues.
Today no double-calling, carolling magpie,

no soloing, mellow-fluting currawong,
or piping butcherbird, not even a gravelly
rumbling of thunderous summer air. Today

only mono-vowelled intonations of misery
and pity slow-tracking with loneliness and longing.
And none of it, none of it breaking down.

Quasimodo's Lament

Crazed carillonneur, will you ever stop hauling
yourself into the cathedral's dim vaults?
Will you ever stop imagining Esmeralda's hands
running along the canted bones of your spine

as if they were feeling the curve of a well-cast
bell? Foolish to think she might one day stroke
your shoulders, caress your hair – still you put
out claim after claim, still you seek to sharpen

your hopes, the clapper's cool aim; still you play
the sallying game, cavernously ringing changes
into the air. Ludicrous rope-lugger, who could

love that stone-hard knur? Will your heart forever
be at peals? You burnish each bell and you ring
them for her: Minstrel, Silverskirr, Gypsyspiel.

Bandit

(1999–2016)

I'm grieving for your bobbing, breeze-buoyed nose
that on your walks would sift the air for the mealy,
leather bases of other dogs' urine in the grass.
I'm grieving for your ears, and though in your old age
they became stuck to silence like leaves against wet glass,
I loved the way you understood our hand-shaped
messages about food, bed, or bath. I loved your tongue

and its wet remittances when I'd carry you, play,
bring you food, or just lie beside you on the bed.
The tail that wagged in direct relationship to happiness,
the whir of joy whenever we'd arrive home, or when
you so quickly deduced, through some subtlety
of smell or gesture, that you'd be coming with us
for long rides in the car. I loved your oboe-toned bark

summoning me for walks. I loved the way your head
would nudge cushions to the floor if they lay
on your spot on the couch. I'm sorry I scolded you
for catching skinks – my anger as inexplicable to you
as the dropped tails shaping and reshaping in the grass.
Sweet dog, we're still finding your hairs on our clothes.
We're saying your name, as if to summon you home.

Camel

I

There is a name for a camel that drinks
from the watering hole at noon. There is a name
for a camel that drinks at any time; a name
for a camel that drinks once during the day

and once at night. There is a name for a camel
that drinks only once every three weeks
despite walking all day over undulating dunes.
There is a name for a camel that leads other

camels to the watering hole; a name
for a camel that gets thirsty quickly, rushing
to arrive. There is a name for a camel
that doesn't drink from the watering hole

when it's busy, but waits and observes.
There is a name for a camel that is frightened
by anything; a name for a camel that loves
to escape and is difficult to catch; a name

for a camel that walks ahead of the other
camels at a great distance so that it appears
to be fleeing. There is a name for a camel
that is superior to all other camels in all things.

2

But is there a name for a camel whose head,
face and back are hit with an electric prodder
as it struggles to walk up a steep ramp onto
a livestock export ship. Is there a name

for a camel who is crowded into a lorry
with many other camels, all unable to move
and transported for hours on end
without exercise, food, or water. Is there

a name for a camel whose nose is torn from
being pulled around by a ring and made to carry
joyriders for twelve hours in the blazing sun;
a name for a camel forced to trudge over

concrete and tar for nearly a thousand miles
to reach the slaughterhouses where, before
it will be struck with a hammer or machete
and left to die slowly in great pain, spits

and uses all four legs to kick; or a name
for the camel skinned, roasted whole, basted
with the fat from its own hump and stuffed
with dates, spices and served at a wedding feast.

3

The barbarians are at the Camel Garden gate.
They are burning the willow trees, long avenues of shade.
They are throwing tacks, nails and sharp-edged stones

over the grass-covered ground. They are pointing
their anti-camel artillery at everything, even at the chickens,
the egrets and the flies. Any time now they will fire

their shots and proclaim that this is the hour
of Camel Lameness, the day of Camel Blindness
as they throw handfuls of burning sand into camels' eyes.

This is the end, they say, of Camel Peace, the end
of cud-chewing Camel Yoga and Divine Contemplation
as they brandish their knives and grease their mouths

with camel fat. This is the dawn of the Camelmen again.
Everything belongs to the Camelmen now:
the oases, the dunes, every book, every crossroad,

every graveyard. This is the end of Camel
Camaraderie and the common good. Camel humps,
they say, will be their new seats of power, the place

from where they'll chant, sing, plot their kidnappings,
beheadings, attacks, invasions; from where
they'll log into Facebook and broadcast their jihad.

4

Praise to the Coalition of Camels.
Praise to your trek through windblown dust and sand,
storms that would quickly blind us.

Praise to your patience, your carrying
of gifts to the prophets.

Praise to your years crossing the windy steppes,
those obdurate hours under your feet.

Praise to your tracks into wastelands,
into the mapless territories of wolves and lions,
always trudging with little birds on your back.

Praise to your basic knowledge that there is the sun
and there is a moonlit pool at midnight,
that there is peace at the edges of empire.

Praise to a Confederacy of Camels,
a Concordance of Camels, a Convergence
of Camels, a Congress of Camels,
a Council of Camels, a Confabulation of Camels,
a Convocation of Camels, a Consolation of Camels.

5

Camel, I wish cool sand always under your feet.
I wish softness for your leathery mouth: hibiscus,
zucchini flowers, figs – I wish you more than twigs,
thorns, saltbush. I wish for you no more loads

or tourists on your back, only cool sprays
of frankincense and myrrh. I wish for you sweet water
and the juice of early harvest muscatels. I wish
you words free of cunning and bragging, a kind

cameleer who will share his milk tea, who will
forgive the stench of your urine, who will ignore
your bad breath to place kisses on your big-lipped snout
and let you greet him each dawn with Chewbacca

grunts before you blow into his face the way
you always welcome other camels in the herd.
I wish for you sanctuary far from the barbed-wire
stockades owned by sheiks and shipping magnates

who would use whips and riding crops to turn your
loopy gait into winnings on their race tracks. I wish
daily rain upon the earth to settle the dust, moisten
the air for your nostrils, to wash the lashes of your eyes.

Cobra

This snake-charmer's less
a musician, more of a scribe
scrawling
his flute through the air –
no musical riffs
only an endless redoodling
of glyphs. I'd like to see
the snake breach type
break the loops
exact a new script
and imprint quick cursive
in the dirt – no longer
a stylus ratifying
its own capture
no longer transcribing
on every street corner
the man's cramped oeuvre.

As Wasps Fly Upwards

I'm walking home in the dying light of a summer's day.
I do not know that within the minute
a tiny beetle will veer into my left eye,
its blade-like parts meant for slicing plant tissue,
slicing my cornea.
I do not know that within an hour
my eye will feel as though it has undergone a corneal graft
with razor blades, burning match heads
and acid rinses – *Christmas eye,* a doctor will call it.

I'm remembering this
because I'm reading about entomologist, Justin Schmidt,
who once clung to a tree
suspended over a Costa Rican gorge
while enraged wasps squirted venom into his eyes;
a man stung by more winged insects than anyone,
who has classified all the piercing, irreverent,
bold, electric, smoky aches down to precise
decimal gradations
on a five-point Sting Pain Index.
I've also been reading a study that describes how Catholics
feel the ferocity of pain ease
if they contemplate images of Mary;
atheists if they watch documentaries
featuring David Attenborough – so I wonder,
when Schmidt steps on a nest of red harvester ants

and pain shoots like mordant dye through his body,
what angelic or analgesic image does he conjure
to demobilise the piercing, crunching agony;
or can he just sigh
and look into the distance and let his mind find relief
in the palliative cotton of windblown clouds?

I recall, once or twice in childhood, the pencil-point pressure
of a fang shooting an aggregation
of misery along my arm
as a spider discharged its voltage before dropping from my wrist
like decommissioned fuse wire.
And then there are the pangs that spasmodically flare
along the nerves on the underside of my upper right arm –
and I wonder if this is like the pain
Schmidt feels in his fingers
when digging up a colony of fire ants.

I remember, too, when an abundance of work and worry
has made my cranium feel as if it belonged
to a large-headed baby undergoing hours of obstructed labour.
Though perhaps if I'd been bitten by a bullet ant –
which Schmidt likens to *fire-walking over flaming charcoal*
with a three-inch rusty nail
grinding into your heel – I might have a better point
of comparison and without hesitation
be grateful I've never had to invent a pain scale,
drawing and quartering metaphors for the way toxins

can burst open cellular membranes, or for the way
suffering can be internally transacted,
made dangerous and monstrous
by the fallacies of the self.

Sometimes I lie awake at night and remember
that death will come – perhaps, suddenly, from a tree
or an overhanging rock, or from a sliding shadow
in the grass; or from a knot of dark blood
bivouacking in my brain.
Or perhaps from a fever, my skin crawling
as though I were lying in the path of a horde of bull acacia ants;
or intense itching and burning as if I'd been
rubbed with a concoction of wasabi, hot mustard
and the necrotising venom of a white tail spider.
Or perhaps, just from a build up over the years
of light, ephemeral stings –
barely noticed, no pain worth recording –
just a remote hum in a honey-vault of light,
then a smoky drifting away.

Notes

The Domesticity of Giraffes

'The Caterpillars': the Doukhobors were a spiritual Christian religious group of Russian origin. With support from the Canadian government, 7500 moved to Western Canada around 1900. They were pacifists who lived in communes that rejected personal materialism.

Accidental Grace

'Girl on a Rooftop Flying a Kite': was partially inspired by Edward Hirsch's poem 'Man on a Fire Escape' published in *Best American Poetry 1992*, ed. Charles Simic, Collier Books, Macmillan Publishing Company. I have adapted some of Hirsch's images and the opening one and a half lines.

'The Elephant Odes': part 4 was inspired by a passage in Donald Hall's poem 'The Black-Faced Sheep' published in *The One Day and Poems 1947–1990*, Carcanet, 1991. The passage is: 'You were not shrewd like the pig./ You were not strong like the horse./ You were not brave like the rooster.'

Wolf Notes

'The Lake': the italicised phrase 'like little electric fig seeds' is from a poem by Charles Wright from his book *Chicamauga*, Noonday, 1995.

'Wolf Notes: 2': partially inspired by Pimone Triplett's poem, 'Self-Portrait as a Dream of Giving up the Child' – section 3, from *Ruining the Picture*, Triquarterly Books,1998). I have adapted some images in the opening lines.

Storm and Honey

The phrase 'storm and honey' comes from Kenneth Slessor's poem 'Captain Dobbin': 'for they were shipmates, too,/ companions of no cruise by reading-glass,/ but fellows of storm and honey from the past' published in *Collected Poems*, ed. by Dennis Haskell and Geoffrey Dutton, Angus and Robertson, 1994, p.77, line 94.

'The Shark': the first two lines are adapted from Dave Smith's 'The Shark in the Rafters', published in *Night Pleasures, New and Selected Poems,* Bloodaxe Books, 1992. Dave Smith's lines are: 'Under the stuttered snatch of the winch/ they draw him up by pulley and wheel.'

'Gale': some images in this poem were suggested to me from passages in *The Perfect Storm* by Sebastian Junger, Harper Perennial, 2006.

'The Harbour': the poem of Robert Gray's I refer to is 'Late Ferry' published in *Cumulus*, John Leonard Press, 2012.

'The Aquarium': the quoted lines are the first stanza of James Galvin's poem 'Girl without Her Nightgown' published in *The Best American Poetry 2008*, ed. by Charles Wright, Scribner Poetry, 2008.

New Poems

'The Boathouse': the line by John Burnside is 'homing/ in on the purer urgency/ of elsewhere' from his poem 'Geese' published in *The Asylum Dance,* Jonathan Cape, 2000.

'Grasses': the line in Stanza 5, 'Yes, earth is the best place for love.' is a response to Robert Frost's line: 'Earth's the right place for love/ I don't know where it's likely to go better.' from his poem 'Birches'.

'Sugarcane Juice': the quote from Niall Campbell is from his poem 'The Blackbird Singer', in his book *Moontide*, Bloodaxe Books, 2014.

'Peterhead': stanza 4, line 2, 'the town that sinks, sinks us all' I have adapted from Lavinia Greenlaw's 'A town that's sinking sinks us all.' from her poem 'Blues (That's another Sunday over)' from her book *The Casual Perfect,* Faber & Faber, 2011.

'Quasimodo's Lament': partly inspired by Anthony Lawrence's poem 'Quasimodo's Bells' published in *Dreaming in Stone,* Angus and Robertson, 1989. His poem also ends with made-up names of bells: 'Angeltongue, Banshee, Goldenmouth, Sirocco.'

'Camel': In Arabic there are over 1000 names for camels. The first section of the poem has been adapted from information on the website: www.arabglot.com/2011/02/how-many-words-are-there-for-camel-in.html, which lists the Arabic names given to camels for certain characteristics. The third section of the poem which begins 'The barbarians are at the Camel Garden gate.' was suggested to me by Ken Smith's poem 'The Chicken Variations: Last bulletin' which begins 'The barbarians are at the city's throat'. A few other phrases are also adapted from this piece. Ken Smith's poem appears in *Shed: Poems 1980–2001,* Bloodaxe Books, 2002.

'As Wasps Fly Upwards': this title is a variation on the quote from Job 5:7 'Yet man is born unto trouble, as the sparks fly upward.' You can read about Justin Schmidt's Sting Pain Index at scienceblogs.com/retrospectacle/2007/05/16/schmidt-pain-index-which-sting

Acknowledgements

Grateful acknowledgement is made to the editors and publishers of the books in which these poems have previously appeared.

New poems in this collection have been published in: *Antipodes, Australian Poetry Journal, Cordite, Irises: The University of Canberra Vice-Chancellor's International Poetry Prize 2017* (ed. Monica Carroll and Paul Munden), *Island, LOOK, Meanjin, Plumwood Mountain, Prayers for a Secular World, Southerly, The Australian Book Review, The Best Australian Poems 2015* (ed. Geoff Page), *The Best Australian Poems 2016* and *2017* (ed. Sarah Holland-Batt), *The Weekend Australian.*

The poem 'As Wasps Fly Upwards' was awarded *ABR*'s Peter Porter Poetry Prize in 2015. The Poem 'By the Shore' was commissioned by Sarah Couper for the Art Gallery of NSW's magazine *LOOK*, March 2017.

My sincere thanks to Ivor Indyk and the team at Giramondo. Thanks also to my postgraduate students at the University of Sydney from whom I am always learning. Thanks to the Sunday group for valuable feedback and comments on the new poems and also to Peter Boyle. Thanks always to Stephen Edgar for abiding love and support.

Index of poem titles

The Giramondo Publishing Company acknowledges the support of Western Sydney University in the implementation of its book publishing program.

This project has been assisted by the Commonwealth Government through the Australia Council, its arts funding and advisory body.